AF718954

WITHDRAWN

HD
69
I7
R69

Rowthorn, Robert
International big business 1957-1967

A10200 182031

University of Cambridge Department of Applied Economics

OCCASIONAL PAPER 24

International Big Business 1957 – 1967

A study of Comparative Growth

University of Cambridge Department of Applied Economics
Occasional Papers

1 *White-collar Redundancy: a Case Study*, by Dorothy Wedderburn

2 *Railway Workshops: the Problems of Contraction*, by P. Lesley Cook

3 *The Economies of Large-Scale Production in British Industry: an Introductory Study*, by C. Pratten, R.M. Dean and A. Silberston

4 *Redundancy and the Railwaymen*, by Dorothy Wedderburn

5 *Parking Space for Cars: Assessing the Demand*, by G.J. Roth

6 *Wage Trends, Wage Policies and Collective Bargaining: the Problems for Underdeveloped Countries*, by H.A. Turner

7 *Growth, Profitability and Valuation: A study of United Kingdom Quoted Companies*, by A. Singh and G. Whittington, in collaboration with H.T. Burley

8 *Productivity in Distribution*, by K.D. George

9 *Industrial Relations in a British Car Factory*, by Garfield Clack

10 *Growth Rate Tables*, by H.T. Burley

11 *The Sterling Area, the Commonwealth and World Economic Growth*, by J.O.N. Perkins

12 *Effects of U.K. Direct Investment Overseas: An Interim Report*, by W.B. Reddaway, in collaboration with J.O.N. Perkins, S.J. Potter and C.T. Taylor

13 *Fortran Programs for Economists*, by Lucy Joan Slater

14 *Demarcation Rules in Shipbuilding and Shiprepairing*, by Geoffrey Roberts

15 *Effects of U.K. Direct Investment Overseas: Final Report*, by W.B. Reddaway, in collaboration with S.J. Potter and C.T. Taylor

16 *Productivity and Capital Expenditure in Retailing*, by K.D. George, in collaboration with P.V. Hills

17 *Productivity in Transport*, by B.M. Deakin and T. Seward

18 *Poverty in Britain and the Reform of Social Security*, by A.B. Atkinson

19 *The Return to Gold 1925: The Formulation of Economic Policy and its Critics*, by D.E. Moggridge

20 *Is Britain Really Strike-Prone?* by H.A. Turner

21 *The Monopolies Commission in Action*, by A. Sutherland

24 *International Big Business 1957–67*, by Robert Rowthorn, in collaboration with S. Hymer

International Big Business 1957–1967
A Study of Comparative Growth

by Robert Rowthorn
Fellow of King's College, Cambridge
in collaboration with
Stephen Hymer

CAMBRIDGE
AT THE UNIVERSITY PRESS
1971

Published by
the Syndics of the Cambridge University Press
Bentley House, 200 Euston Road, London N.W.1
American Branch: 32 East 57th Street, New York, N.Y.10022

© Department of Applied Economics, University of Cambridge 1971

Library of Congress Catalogue Card Number: 70–14 2963

ISBNS: 0 521 08113 0 clothbound
0 521 09641 3 paperback

This book has been set in cold type by E.W.C. Wilkins and Associates Ltd. London, and printed in Great Britain by Alden & Mowbray Ltd. Oxford.

Contents

Tables

Preface

This book is the result of further work on an earlier pilot study by Stephen Hymer and myself which appeared under the title 'The Multinational Corporation: The Non-American Challenge' (in: *The International Corporation*, ed. C.P. Kindleberger, Harvard 1970). The original classification of firms into industries and much of the econometric analysis has been untilised here. In this sense the book is a joint effort. There is another sense in which this is true. Countless discussions during Stephen Hymer's visits to England have created a common approach to the large firm and to the particular problems discussed here.

I should like to thank those who read parts or the whole of various drafts. John Eatwell and Geoffrey Whittington made long and detailed criticisms, many of which were accepted. Brian Van Arkadie edited an initially incomprehensible text. Without his efforts this book would never have appeared. Prabat Patnaik and Mario Nuti also made valuable comments.

I should also like to thank those who typed the drafts and helped with the computing, in particular, Mrs Barbara Leonard, Mrs Mabel Simmonds, Miss Judith Barnes, and Mrs Roberta Coe.

1. Introduction

1. The American challenge

One of the most striking features of the capitalist world during the last quarter century has been the massive overseas expansion of American firms, particularly in manufacturing and allied industries which have come to account for the bulk of US direct investments abroad. Much of this investment has gone tc other advanced economies where American firms now account for significant shares of production. A few statistics will illustrate the scale of this expansion. Within seventeen years, between 1950 and 1967, US manufacturing and petroleum investments in Europe rose more than tenfold from $1,358 million to $14,185 million.[1] In Canada over the same period they rose more than fivefold from $2,315 million to $11,902 million. By the mid-1960s American firms produced 75 per cent of the computers sold in Europe and an even larger proportion of integrated electronic circuits. Half the pharmaceuticals brought by the British National Health Service were produced by American firms.[2]

Amongst Europeans and other non-Americans, this expansion has evoked the vision of a world dominated by American capital, where non-American capital is forced to accept a subordinate role in growth industries, and is able to maintain its position only in slow-growing and backward sectors. These fears have been forcefully and influentially articulated by the French journalist Jean-Jaques Servan-Schreiber in his book *The American Challenge,* where he says: 'Most striking of all is the *strategic* character of American industrial penetration. One by one, US corporations capture those sectors of the economy most technologically advanced, most adaptable to change, and with the highest growth rates.'[3] and 'Starting with a rather matter-of-fact examination of American investment in Europe, we find an economic system which is in a state of collapse. It is our own. We see a foreign challenger breaking down the political and psychological framework of our societies. We are witnessing the prelude to our own historical bankruptcy.'

Exaggerated as these fears may seem, there is no doubt that they are widely accepted in Europe, where it is believed that the gap between American and non-American firms is increasing. Moreover, Servan-Schreiber's explanations of this allegedly increasing gap are also widely accepted. Christopher Layton, for example, a rather more cautious exponent of these views gives three reasons why American firms are pulling ahead.[4] Firstly, the size of a firm is a crucial factor determining its ability to innovate, and, by implication, its ability to grow. Thus American firms being bigger than their non-American counterparts, with other things being equal, grow faster. Secondly, American firms receive the benefit of the enormous research and development expenditures of the

American government in fields of armaments and space. Finally, American managers being better trained are more skilled than their non-American counterparts.

Once this picture of an overwhelming and increasing American lead and its causes is accepted, it is but a short step to conclude, as do its exponents, that European countries must combine to combat the American colossus. Firms must be encouraged, or even forced, to merge, both within countries and across national boundaries so that they can reap economies of scale. State expenditure on research and development must be increased dramatically and European technical resources pooled. Finally, management and technical training facilities must be greatly expanded.

It is surprising that this description of the problems facing Europe and the measures necessary to overcome them has been so widely and readily accepted, for although some parts of the analysis are undoubtedly correct, others appear to be rather dubious. A casual examination of the evidence suggests that the gap between American and Continental European economies or firms has not changed very much in recent years and that size is not beneficial to growth. Let us examine each of these propositions in turn.

Although output per head is much greater in the United States than in Europe this gap is not widening; on the contrary, it may even be narrowing. Between 1963 and 1968, for example, a period when the American economy grew particularly fast, the ratio of GNP per head in America to GNP per head in the EEC fell from 2.21 to 2.15. This is not a very striking fall, perhaps, but we should not expect it if the American economy was drawing away from the European. When we look at industrial production the picture is the same. In the United States industrial production grew very rapidly in the mid-60's at a time when European growth faltered. Towards the end of the decade, however, the situation was reversed as European growth recovered and American growth came to a standstill. As a result, industrial production at the end of 1969 was 45 per cent higher in the EEC than it had been in 1963 and 38 per cent higher in the US.

Between 1957 and 1963 Continental European firms grew much faster than American firms. According to the American magazine *Fortune*, the number of Continentals amongst the top 200 industrial firms in the world rose from thirty in 1957 to forty-one in 1962 and the number of Americans fell from 135 to 123. During the next six years the position more or less stabilised with the Continentals falling back a little relative to the Americans. In 1969 there were thirty-nine Continentals amongst the top 200 and 128 Americans. This slight improvement in the relative position of the Americans was nowhere near enough to compensate for their slow growth in the earlier period.[5]

Turning to the relationship between size and growth of firms, numerous empirical studies have failed to reveal any systematic relation between average growth rates and size. Large firms tend to have more uniform growth rates than small firms, but their average growth rates seem to be much the same. There are proportionately fewer slow-growers amongst the large firms, but, equally, there are proportionately fewer fast-growers. Much the same is true of profitability. Large firms do not seem to enjoy higher profit rates than small firms. Their profits do, however, seem to be less variable.

At first sight it might seem that the absence of any systematic relationship between size and growth is inconsistent with the high levels of industrial concentration which characterise advanced capitalist economies. If a few hundred firms now account for the bulk of output, assets, and profits, this might suggest that big firms either are growing or have at some time in the past grown faster than small firms. This need not, however, be so. It is well-known that a succession of random disturbances, quite unrelated to the size of the firm, may eventually lead, no matter what the initial size distribution of firms, to a situation where the sizes of firms have a log-normal distribution similar to the distribution of firms observed today. This is known as 'Gibrat's Law', or the 'law of proportionate effect'. Moreover, the law of proportionate effect will cause the level of concentration to increase steadily over time.[6] Thus, purely random factors may cause the share of large firms to rise steadily over time, and may lead to a distribution of sizes similar to that which we observe today. It is incorrect, therefore, to take existing levels of concentration or even a tendency for these levels to increase, as evidence that big firms on average, grow, or have grown, faster than small firms.

2. The growth of firms: size, nationality and industry

The evidence we have just discussed suffers from a number of limitations.

The comparisons of European and American growth rates were based upon highly aggregated measures such as total industrial production, or the number of firms of a given nationality in the top 200. Such comparisons are an inadequate way of testing the hypothesis that American firms are growing faster than European firms in modern technologically advanced industries, for the overall equality of European and American growth might be the result of two opposite development patterns. European firms might be growing faster in traditional industries, whereas American firms could be growing faster in modern industries. In so far as the American Challenge concerns the latter industries, the performance of European firms in traditional industries is irrelevant.

The evidence on growth and size, referred to above comes from one or other of two kinds of study. In the first, the industry or country to which a firm belongs is ignored, and the overall or average relationship between size and growth is estimated. For reasons discussed briefly in Chapter 4, this procedure may lead to incorrect conclusions. The second kind of study restricts itself to the firms of one industry and one country. Each industry is usually so narrowly defined that it contains only a few large firms. The bulk are small and medium-sized, with the result that the conclusions reflect the growth experience of these firms rather than that of large firms. Now, when considering the American Challenge, it is clear that the relationship between size and growth amongst small firms, with sales of say $1 million a year or even $10 million a year, is of secondary importance. What really matters is the relationship amongst firms with sales of the order of $100 million a year or more.

Thus existing evidence is either subject to the drawback that it makes no adequate allowance for systematic differences in growth rates between firms of different countries or industries, or else reflects mainly the experience of small firms. It is necessary to study the relationship between size and growth amongst big firms, and to make some explicit allowance for the effects of nationality and industry on growth.

The ideal way to approach the 'American Challenge' is to place the whole question into a wider context, and examine the relationship between growth, size, nationality and industry amongst large firms. Part I of this book contains an econometric analysis of the growth experiences of the top 500 industrial firms in the capitalist world during 1957–67. The analysis is an extension and consolidation of an earlier pilot study, the results of which were published in an article entitled. *The Multinational Corporation : The Non-American Challenge.*[7]

3. Firms and the national economy

The econometric analysis of Part I quantifies some of the basic components of growth during the years 1957–67. It ascribes the observed differences in the growth rates of firms to differences in nationality, industry or size. However, although eliminating more fanciful theories, this analysis operates at a rather superficial level, for it measures rather than explains international differences in the growth rates of firms. To remedy this defect Part II of this study attempts to relate the growth of firms to the growth of their domestic economies. As with the econometric analysis of Part I, this analysis will carry further some of the ideas in the earlier article which discussed the forces underlying the enormous post-war increase in international investment, the role played by this investment in the growth of large firms, and how this investment affects the relationship between firms and their domestic economies.

A theme of the article was that the growth of large firms is an oligopolistic process in which overseas investment plays an increasingly important part. The long-run prospect is one of interpenetration, whereby the firms of most advanced capitalist countries invest heavily in most other advanced capitalist countries. This interpenetration will have two effects. It will weaken the links binding firms to their domestic economies by raising the proportion of their activities conducted abroad, and it will help large firms based on slow-growing economies by enabling them to shift their activities towards fast-growing economies. Each of these will be reflected in declining correlation between the growth rates of large firms and the growth rates of national economies.

Part II does not seek to extend or modify this admittedly rudimentary analys[is] but, rather, to lend it more substance by spelling out certain parts of it which were left implicit, and to put it into perspective by quantifying much of what was originally qualitative. The relationship between the growth of firms and the growth of national economies, for example, is discussed in some detail. This involves considering how the growth of firms may be affected by changes in the level of domestic concentration or by expansion overseas. It also involves considering how the growth of firms will be affected by losses in the domestic economy to foreign firms. In this discussion the growth rates of national economies are taken to be exogenously determined variables, and no attempt is made to explain them. The causation, such as it is, runs from national economies to firms rather than *vice versa* or, to put the matter differently, from macro to micro. In reality, of course, the historical process has been one of interaction in which the behaviour of economies has both influenced and been influenced by the behaviour of firms. Such interactions are not, however, discussed.

As in the econometric analysis, the emphasis is quantitative throughout. Attempts are made to estimate:

(1) the importance of overseas expansion to manufacturing firms during the period under consideration,

(2) the extent to which overseas expansion was a two-way process of interpenetration, in which firms of each country lost part of their home economy to foreigners at the same time as they gained access to foreign economies,

(3) the correlation between the growth rates of large firms and growth rates of their national economies,

(4) and, finally, the relative importance to American firms of the growth of the American economy, changes in their share of that economy, and overseas expansion.

Although these estimates are crude they give us an idea of how far the predicted weakening of the links between firms and their national economies has actually taken place, how far firms based on slow-growing economies have been able to keep up with those based on fast-growing economies, and how far they will be able to do so in the future. They also help us put the 'American Challenge' into perspective.

Part I. The Growth of firms: size, nationality and industry

2. The data

1. Introduction

In this chapter the data used for the regression analysis of future chapters and its drawbacks and limitations are described. The measures used for the size of firm, biasses arising from the choice of samples, and problems raised by mergers are also discussed.

2. The sources

The most comprehensive and readily accessible sources of data on the sales, assets, profits, and employment of large corporations are the annual directories published by the American magazine *Fortune*. In all but a few cases, their data are derived from material either published by the firms themselves or communicated privately to *Fortune*.

Initially the directories contained only information on US firms but were soon extended to include non-US firms and, later, to include even more of the latter. As a result information is now available on the 500 largest US industrial firms[1] from 1954 to the present, on the 100 largest non-US industrial firms from 1956 to 1962 and on the 200 largest non-US industrial firms from 1962 onwards.

Despite their imperfections, particularly in the case of non-US firms, these statistics, when adjusted in simple and obvious ways, provide a useful starting point for an analysis of the performance of big firms.

3. The samples

The nature of the samples and the time periods covered were more or less determined by the basic aims of the analysis: to measure the relative performance of the big firms of various countries and discover how far observed differences could be statistically explained by such factors as the size, industry, and nationality of these firms.

Given these aims the *Fortune* data as they stand pose certain problems. In the earlier years, particularly, coverage of US firms is far wider than of non-US firms. The former are both more numerous than the latter and extend lower down on the size scale. In 1961, for example, there were 500 US firms in the list, of which the 500th had sales of $76 million. By contrast there were 100 non-US firms, of which the smallest had sales of $294 million. It is clear that any analysis based upon all of these firms would have risked being swamped by the Americans.

To overcome this problem we decided to look at two time periods of equal length 1957–62 and 1962–7, and to exclude enough US firms in each period to ensure that the others were not swamped.

1962–7

For the period 1962–7 we excluded all US firms whose sales in 1962 were less than those of the smallest non-US firm. This gave us initially 300 US and 200 non-US firms, or in other words the 500 largest firms in the capitalist world.[2]

Some of these firms disappeared from the *Fortune* directory during the period. A few, present in 1962, grew too slowly and were pushed out of the directory by fast-growing newcomers. Others took part in mergers in which they were taken-over or merged into some bigger unit. Many of these merged firms were dropped from the sample but others, as we shall see below, were included. After the various exclusions a total of 438 firms is left, of which 280 are American and 158 are non-American, or in percentage terms 64 per cent and 36 per cent respectively. This sample we shall call the *full sample.*

Thus some twenty US and forty-two non-US firms were dropped. One reason for the US figure being both relatively and absolutely smaller is *Fortune's* much greater coverage of US firms. Since there are 500 places in the US list, a slowly growing US firm could drop out of the top 300 and yet remain listed for some years amongst the remaining 200. Indeed seventeen US firms did exactly this, and were, therefore, included in the sample.[3] By contrast their non-US equivalents disappeared from the *Fortune* lists altogether, and were, therefore, dropped from the sample.

By including seventeen slow-growing US firms, yet excluding their non-US equivalents, the relative growth rate of non-US firms has been biassed upwards, particularly in the food and miscellaneous categories which account for 12 of the 17. It is explained in Appendix 1, however, that no method was without its disadvantages.

1957–62

The problems posed by the period 1957–62 are rather different. No non-US firm in the top 100 in 1957 grew so slowly that if failed to qualify for the top 200 in 1957. Thus the biasses just discussed were absent in this period. On the other hand, to have followed the procedure used for the later period, and included all US firms with sales in 1957 greater than or equal to those of the smallest non-US firm (100th) in 1957, would have meant swamping the sample with US firms. Out of an initial sample, before exclusions, of 330 some 230 would have been American.

In the absence of any clear alternative criterion it was decided, arbitrarily, to include only the top 100 US firms in 1957. After various exclusions we ended up with ninety-seven US firms and seventy-seven non-US firms, or in other words 44 per cent of our sample consisted of non-American firms. This sample we shall call the *reduced sample.*

Mergers, ineradicable changes in the data, and various other factors accounted for many of the exclusions. The biggest single cause, however, was the elimination of ten firms which, although they survived the period 1957–62, failed to survive the following period 1962–67. These firms were excluded because the earlier period was not analysed so much in its own right, but more as a standard of comparison for the later period. We wanted, therefore, to include only firms which continued throughout the entire ten years, thereby enabling us to compare the behaviour of the same sample of firms in the two periods. Fortunately regressions based on a sample which included the ten firms gave much the same results as the present sample.

The samples used

Thus, the samples used are:

(*A*). The full sample with an upward bias in non-US growth rates, and an upward bias in the growth rates of small firms.

(*B*). A slightly smaller sample, derived from the full sample by eliminating the 17 slow growing US firms. This is without a non-US bias but has a larger upward bias in the growth rates of small firms.

(*C*). A considerably smaller sample, from which the biasses are eliminated but the already small number of non-US firms is reduced by about a half.

These samples are summarised in Table 1.

Table 1: *Biasses caused by deletion for the period 1962–7*

	Sample size	Non-US bias	Small firm bias
Sample A (full sample)	438	+	+
Sample B	421	0	++
Sample C (reduced sample)	174	0	0

For the period 1962–7 we were concerned to get as large a sample of non-US firms as possible, and were interested in the effects of both size and nationality on growth rates; all three of the methods were used, therefore. When the object was to study the effects of size on growth Sample A, which gave a large sample with a moderate bias, and Sample C, which gave a small sample without bias, were used. These correspond to the full and the reduced samples respectively. When American firms are considered on their own, Sample A gives an unbiassed estimate of the effects of size on growth. Where the object was to study international differences in growth rates Samples B and C were used, each of which gives a sample without bias.

For 1957–62 and 1957–67 we were compelled to use only the reduced sample, which is free of bias.

4. Industry and country classification

Firms were classified both by industry and nationality with results shown in Table 2.

In this classification food was assumed to include drink, but not tobacco, which was put into miscellaneous. Detergents were included under chemicals.[4] Non-electrical engineering and iron and steel were difficult to distinguish, particularly in Europe where firms operate in both sectors.[5] Finally, conglomerates, which have received so much attention in recent years, were mostly too small in 1962 to be included in the sample and, therefore, the problem of classifying them by industry did not have to be solved.

Table 2 *Number of firms by nationality and industry, 1957–62 (and 1957–67). The reduced sample.*

	US	Germany	France	Benelux	Italy	UK	Other EFTA	Japan	Canada	Other	World total	Non-US	Europe	Continental Europe
Food	12	–	–	–	–	5	1	–	1	1	20	8	6	1
Chemicals	11	4	–	1	1	3	1	–	–	–	21	10	10	7
Oil	16	–	1	1	–	2	–	–	–	–	20	4	4	2
Iron and steel	8	4	2	2	–	4	–	2	1	–	23	15	12	8
Non-ferrous	7	–	–	–	–	–	–	–	2	1	10	3	–	–
Engineering (ex. electrical)	6	3	–	–	–	3	1	1	1	–	15	9	7	4
Electrical	9	2	–	1	–	4	2	–	–	–	18	9	9	5
Autos	4	2	3	–	1	3	1	–	–	–	14	10	10	7
Miscellaneous	24	–	2	–	1	6	–	–	–	–	33	9	9	3
Total	97	15	8	5	3	30	6	3	5	2	174	77	67	37

Number of firms by nationality and industry, 1962–7. The full sample.

	US	Germany	France	Benelux	Italy	UK	Other EFTA	Japan	Canada	Other	World total	Non-US	Europe	Continental Europe
Food	44	–	–	–	–	9	1	1	2	1	58	14	10	1
Chemicals	39	7	3	2	2	4	4	5	–	–	66	27	22	18
Oil	21	–	1	1	1	2	–	1	–	1	28	7	5	3
Iron and steel	13	5	3	3	1	4	1	5	1	2	38	25	17	13
Non-ferrous	12	1	1	–	–	1	–	–	2	1	18	6	3	2
Engineering (ex. electrical)	33	5	1	–	–	3	1	4	1	–	48	15	10	7
Electrical	32	3	2	2	1	6	3	6	2	–	57	25	17	11
Autos	17	2	3	–	1	4	1	5	–	–	33	16	11	7
Miscellaneous	69	1	4	–	1	13	–	2	2	–	92	23	19	6
Total	280	24	18	8	7	46	11	29	10	5	438	158	114	68

In the country classification the only problem was deciding upon the nationality of two Anglo-Dutch firms; eventually both were classified as British.[6]

5. Sales as a measure of size

The *Fortune* directories contain four sets of statistics which can be used as a measure of the size of firms and from which growth rates can be computed: employees, net profits, assets, and sales. Each of these has its own advantages and disadvantages and which of them is appropriate depends upon the purpose for which size and growth rates are required. The aim was to analyse the changing relative position of firms as actual or potential competitors on a world-wide level. Let us, therefore, examine each of these measures with this in mind.

Employees is clearly unsuitable for it takes no account of the wide variations in labour productivity both between countries, and over time. Capital deepening and technical progress, which account for much of the difference in the relative performance of firms, would be completely ignored by this measure.

Net profits are disqualified on the grounds that they are extremely difficult to compare internationally because of differences in accounting practice. In the words of the *Fortune* directory for 1958: 'However, it must be noted that the profits listed are those reported by the companies themselves. In many cases they bear little resemblance to real earnings, because some countries do not require corporations to divulge their profits to stockholders. Thus, to cite a few examples, the earnings reported by Nestlé, Siemens, and Michelin are believed to be only one-quarter to one-third of actual profits.' Moreover, profits vary widely from year to year and the growth rate of profits between two given years is likely to give little indication of the overall performance of a firm.

Assets are a rather better measure, although variations in accounting practices and in the price of intermediate goods make comparisons between countries and even between firms hazardous. Growth rates are likely to be distorted by periodic revaluations, and even by changes in the degree of capacity utilisation.[7]

Sales, as the only real rival to assets, have the disadvantage of being dependent on the degree of vertical integration of the firm. When size comparisons are made between industries with widely different degrees of integration, value-added, – which measures better the production of firms, – is likely to diverge significantly from sales. Within industries or when growth rates are being considered, however, this divergence is not likely to be very important. Moreover, from our point of view, which emphasises market position, sales is a better guide than value-added, since firms will be more concerned with their rivals' sales than with their value-added.[8]

Other drawbacks in the use of sales are the shifting conventions by which excise taxes, import duties, consolidations and the like are treated. In one year, for example, import duties may be included and in the next they may not. Unless some adjustment is made the resulting growth rate will differ from the true one. Equally, exchange-rate changes may not be enough to compensate for differing rates of inflation in various countries. Fortunately, most of these distortions were not too serious in the period under consideration and, as a rule, compensating adjustments were possible.

On balance, sales seem to provide a more reliable measure of size than employees, assets or profits.

6. Mergers, adjustments and deletions

Mergers

During the second time-period, in particular, a number of mergers between firms in the *Fortune* lists occurred, Unfortunately, economic theory does not give any clear guidance on how mergers should be treated. One approach is to assume that the largest firm increases its sales through the addition of the sales of those with which it merges during the time-period, and to regard the other firms as 'deaths' which can either be dropped from the sample, or else given some arbitrary growth rate such as – 100 per cent for the period as a whole. Alternatively, the firms can be considered as if they had constituted one single unit throughout the whole period. Thus the growth rate of their combined sales is computed. Finally the combined sales of the merged firms at the end of the period can be split up in proportion to the sales of the constituent firms at the time they merged. Each firm can then be included in the sample as though it had never merged.

Since it was impractical to use all of these methods it was decided to adopt two of them, which can be described mathematically as follows.

Suppose firms numbered 1 ... r merge into one unit. Let S_0^j $(j = 1 \dots r)$ denote the sales of firm j at the beginning of the period. Let S_1 denote the total sales of the merged firms at the end of the period. Finally suppose that $S_0^1 \geqq S_0^j$ for $j = 2 \dots r$.

Method 1. Eliminate firms 2 ... r from the sample. Assign to firm 1 the growth rate:

$$\left(\frac{S_1}{S_0^1}\right)^{1/n} - 1,$$

where n is the number of years in the period.

Method 2. Eliminate firms 2 ... r from the sample. Assign to firm 1 the growth rate:

$$\left(\frac{S_1}{S_0^1 + \dots + S_0^r}\right)^{1/n} - 1.$$

Which of these two methods is preferable is open to dispute. Method 1 clearly assigns a very high growth rate to merging firms, as in the case of the US oil industry whose firms achieved spectacular growth rates by merging during the years 1962–7. Yet this may better represent the effects of mergers on oligopolistic rivalry than a method which eliminates the effect of mergers entirely. In jockeying for leadership in an industry a firm may be concerned about the size of its immediate rivals. If, on the other hand, a firm is interested only in its market share, and does not regard the size of its immediate rivals as important, Method 2 will be appropriate.

Method 2 has one drawback. To eliminate completely the effects of mergers it would be necessary to know the details of every merger in which firms in our samples took part. Unfortunately, *Fortune* gives details of mergers only when both firms concerned were on the list at the time. A merger between a firm on the list and another off the list is not mentioned. Thus it is not possible to apply Method 2 in its entirety and instead a modified version, in which only the effects of mergers between firms on the *Fortune* lists are removed, must be used. As we explain in Appendix 1, this modified version can, in principle, lead to biasses. Fortunately, they seem to be considerably smaller than those caused by the deletion of small slowly growing firms.

During the period 1962–7 a total of 37 firms in our sample took part in mergers with other firms on the *Fortune* list. Of these 28 were US firms and 8 were non-US. In two industries mergers were significant: oil, where 8 out of 21 US firms were affected, and non-US iron and steel, where 3 out of 13 were affected.

In the preceding period 1957–62, however, only six firms in our sample were affected by mergers. Such a small number did not justify using both of the methods just described, and, therefore, only the second method, i.e., the growth rate of combined sales, is used.

Thus for 1962–7 two different ways of dealing with mergers are adopted and for 1957–62 only one.

Adjustments and deletions

Quite apart from the distortions caused by mergers the data suffered from several other defects. In the earlier years, in particular, some firms did not publish sales figures, with the result that *Fortune* was compelled to estimate them, sometimes with and sometimes without the help of the firms concerned. Changing methods of consolidation provided another source of error, as did the changing treatment of various taxes. Finally, a nation-wide copper strike caused the sales of US copper firms to dip sharply in 1967.

These various defects in the data were handled by using first of all information given in the footnotes in *Fortune*. Then, to evade the effects of the US copper strike, by using different time period for the non-ferrous metals industry. Annual growth rates were computed for the period 1962–6.

Next, we went through the entire set of year to year changes to see if there were any major shifts in a firm's ranking still unexplained. Some of these shifts were obviously of a genuine kind, due either to a cycle or a trend. These were left unaltered. A few, however, were obviously of a statistical nature. The sales of these firms, for all available years, were plotted and crude graphical adjustments made. In the case of firms in 1957–62, however, no reliable adjustment could be made by this method and the firms were dropped.

Altogether the following adjustments and deletions were made:

1962–7

(a) The US copper strike. Adjustments were made to the sales of eighteen firms.

(b) Consolidations, tax changes, faulty estimates, etc. Adjustments were made to the sales of eleven firms.

1957–62

(a) Miscellaneous faults in the data. No adjustments but four deletions.

The two methods

Rather than attempt to combine all the various ways of treating mergers, with all the various ways of treating the data, two basic methods were chosen.

Unadjusted data consist of crude *Fortune* data without any of the adjustments discussed in the last section. Mergers have been treated according to Method 1, i.e. they have been regarded as takeovers by the firm with the largest opening size.

Adjusted data consist of *Fortune* data adjusted as described in the previous section. Mergers have been treated according to Method 2, i.e. the growth rate of the combined assets has been used.

As there were so few mergers or adjustments during the earlier period the results based on unadjusted data for the years 1957–62 have not been included.

7. Summary

This chapter has described the data together with their limitations and the attempts made to overcome these. The largest or *full* sample consists roughly of the 500 biggest industrial firms in the capitalist world as given by the magazine *Fortune*. Of these 300 are American and the remainder non-American. Information on the size, and, therefore, growth rates of these firms is available for 1962–7 but not for 1957–62. For the earlier period a smaller or *reduced* sample is used consisting of the 100 largest Americans and the 100 largest non-Americans. Firms are classified into ten 'countries' and nine industries. Consolidated sales, including those of overseas subsidiaries, are taken as a measure of size. Where the data on sales does not seem satisfactory adjustments are made. This may lead to biasses. A more important source of bias, however, is the limited coverage of the *Fortune* lists, which contain fewer non-American than American firms.

Of the various ways of treating the data, two were chosen which gave rise to *unadjusted* data and *adjusted* data. The results based on both kinds of data will be given for the period 1962–7. In the earlier period the two kinds differed so little that only the results based on adjusted data will be given for 1957–62 and 1957–67.

3. The method of analysis

1. Introduction

This chapter describes the mathematical models underlying the regression analysis of future chapters. It also describes how some of the results of these regressions can be displayed in a simple and convenient form using the variable Z. Finally, it shows how to test the significance of any estimated value or collection of estimated values of Z.

2. The hypothesis

Certain empirical studies of the growth of the firm have been concerned to test a strong version of the 'law of proportionate effect', stating that the growth of a firm is a random variable whose distribution is log-normal and is independent of the size of the firm. Mathematically, this may be expressed by the equation,

$$\log(1 + g) = u, \quad (1)$$

where g is the growth rate and u is normally distributed and independent of size.

To test how far growth is independent of size it is usual to add a function of size ($f(S)$) to the right of (1), to give:

$$\log(1 + g) = f(S) + u. \quad (2)$$

When g is small, as it is in the present case, we can, without serious error, replace $\log(1 + g)$ by g to give the following more convenient version of (2):[1]

$$g = f(S) + u. \quad (3)$$

If the population of firms is reasonably homogeneous, so that there are no large systematic forces at work, Equations (2) and (3) may be fairly close to the truth, for the Central Limit Theorem will ensure that u is normally distributed. In the present case, however, the population is far from homogeneous and there are large systematic variations in rates of growth between one industry and another, and between one country and another. The error may not, therefore, be normally distributed. More seriously, industry and nationality may be correlated with size, so that the error term may not be independent. Any estimate we derive from an equation of the form (3) may reflect the influence of industry or nationality on growth, rather than size. There is, however, a more fundamental reason for being dissatisfied with formulations of the kind given by Equation (3). Our purpose is to see how far each of the factors size, nationality, and, to a lesser extent, industry have affected growth. It is not satisfactory, therefore, to treat industry and nationality as random variables whose effects are included amongst the errors.

One alternative would be to examine separately the firms of each particular country and industry. Using subscripts i and j to indicate that we are restricting ourselves to firms from country i and industry j, we should then fit curves of the form,

$$g_{ij} = f_{ij}(S) + u_{ij}. \tag{4}$$

Unfortunately this method is not practicable in this case, for it means fitting an extremely large number of separate curves. There are 10 countries and 9 industries, giving 90 curves in all. Yet the largest sample contains only 438 firms, or an average of less than 5 firms per country – industry cell. Many of the cells are empty. Only 6 out of 10 countries had food firms in the sample, for example, in 1962–7. Or, to take another example, there were only 6 Italian firms spread between 5 industries.

As a more practicable alternative we may assume that some or all of the functions f_{ij} are related to each other in a systematic way. This will enable us to pool the firms of some, or even all, industries or countries into one sample, which can be used to estimate a number of f_{ij}'s simultaneously.

Independent effects

The simplest such assumption is that country, industry and size all have their own influence on growth, and that these influences are independent of each other. A firm's rate of growth g will then be composed of three systematic parts – a 'country effect' α_i, an 'industry effect' β_j, and a 'size effect' $f(S)$ – together with an unsystematic or random part u_{ij}. The equations (4) can now be written as:

$$g_{ij} = \alpha_i + \beta_j + f(S) + u_{ij}, \tag{5}$$

which can be rewritten as one single equation,

$$g = \sum_{i=1}^{m} \alpha_i C_i + \sum_{j=1}^{n} \beta_j I_j + f(S) + u, \tag{6}$$

where C_j, I_j are dummy variables such that $C_i = 1$ for a firm in the ith country and 0 otherwise, and $I_j = 1$ for a firm in the jth industry and 0 otherwise. To estimate this function some explicit form must be chosen for $f(S)$. The choice is necessarily arbitrary. In the following pages we shall rely mainly on the functional form $f(S) = c \log S + d \log^2 S$, which is convenient, although not intrinsically superior to a number of other functional forms which spring to mind.[2] As a check other forms were also tried and, where interesting, results derived from these forms have been included.

In our basic functional form a firm from country i and industry j will have a growth rate given by $g = \alpha_i + \beta_i + c \log S + d \log^2 S + u_{ij}$. Curves of this are illustrated in Figs. 1(a) and 1(b).

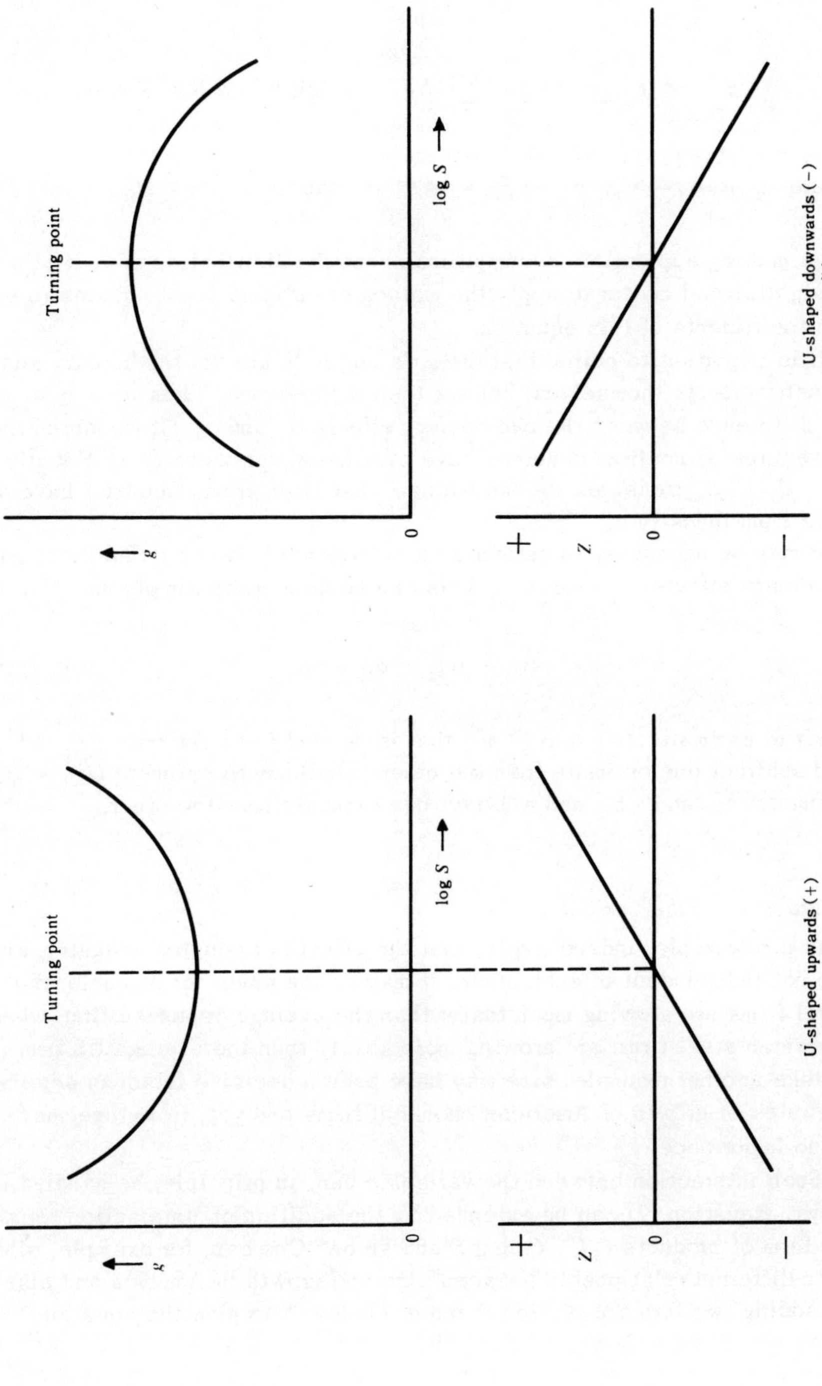

Fig. 1 g and Z as functions of $\log S$.

For econometric reasons, we exclude the dummies of an arbitrary country (US) and an arbitrary industry (miscellaneous), which we assume to be country 1 and industry n respectively.[3] Having done this we arrive at the following equation

$$g = e + \sum_{i=2}^{m} a_i C_i + \sum_{j=1}^{n-1} b_j I_j + c \log S + d \log^2 S + u, \qquad (7)$$

where $a_i = \alpha_i - \alpha_1$, $b_j = \beta_j - \beta_n$, and the $e = \alpha_1 + \beta_n$.

After making appropriate assumptions about the distribution of u, it is a straightforward matter to apply the method of ordinary least squares to estimate the coefficients of this equation.

It is important to notice that the a_i's and b_j's are not the country and industry effects themselves, but are their *differences*. Thus $a_i = \alpha_i - \alpha_1$ is the difference between the two country effects α_i and α_1. It measures the 'advantage' firms from country i have over firms from country 1. Equally $b_j = \beta_j - \beta_n$ measures the 'advantage' that firms from industry j have over firms from industry n.

It may be necessary to estimate the difference between an arbitrary pair of country effects α_{i_1} and α_{i_2}. This can be done quite simply as

$$\alpha_{i_1} - \alpha_{i_2} = a_{i_1} - a_{i_2}$$

Thus to estimate $(\alpha_{i_1} - \alpha_{i_2})$ all that is needed is to estimate a_{i_1} and a_{i_2}, and subtract one estimate from the other. Similarly to estimate $(\beta_{j_1} - \beta_{j_2})$, estimate b_{j_1} and b_{j_2} and subtract one estimate from the other.

Interaction of the variables

It is conceivable, indeed likely, that the effects of country, industry, and size are not independent of each other. It may be the case, for example, that Japane steel firms are growing much faster than the average Japanese firm, whereas American steel firms are growing more slowly than the average US firm. Or, to take another example, size may have been a decisive factor in determining the rates of growth of American chemical firms and yet, in Europe, have been of no importance.

Such interaction between the variables can, in principle, be handled in two ways. Equation (7) can be extended by the addition of 'interaction terms' in the form of products $C_i I_j$, $C_i \log S$ and so on. One can, for example, allow for a different relationship between size and growth in America and elsewhere, by adding two terms $c_1 C_1 \log S$ and $d_1 C_1 \log^2 S$ to give the equation:

$$g = e + \sum_{i=2}^{m} a_i C_i + \sum_{j=1}^{n-1} b_j I_j + (c + c_1 C_1) \log S +$$

$$+ (d + d_1 C_1) \log^2 S + u. \tag{8}$$

This method is often impractical as it can result in equations containing fifty or even more explanatory variables. The alternative is to go back some way towards the original formulation of Equation (4), and restrict ourselves to the firms of a group of countries or industries. Many of our results are, for example, derived from *industry* regressions in which firms are grouped into four 'countries' – the US, the UK, Continental Europe, and Japan – to give for any industry j an equation of the following form:

$$g_j = e_j + a_{j\mathrm{UK}} C_{\mathrm{UK}} + a_{j\mathrm{EU}} C_{\mathrm{EU}} + a_{j\mathrm{Ja}} C_{\mathrm{Ja}} + c_j \log S + d_j \log^2 S + u_j, \tag{9}$$

where the dummy for the US has been excluded, C_{UK}, C_{Eu}, and C_{Ja} are dummies such that $C_{\mathrm{UK}} = 1$ for UK firms and 0 otherwise, $C_{\mathrm{Eu}} = 1$ for continental European firms and 0 otherwise, and $C_{\mathrm{Ja}} = 1$ for Japanese firms and 0 otherwise.

Miscellaneous problems of specification and estimation

In addition to the problems just discussed, there exist a variety of other questions as to the correct method of specifying the hypothesis or of estimating the various equations. Some of these are dealt with in the text as they arise and others in footnotes. Some of the most important are gathered together in appendices.

3. Exposition

Second-order equations such as (7), (8) or (9) are difficult to interpret unless they are depicted graphically, which is impractical when there are many of them to consider. Moreover, it is difficult to compare a number of such equations. To overcome these problems the results can be presented in a different form, which, once the reader becomes accustomed to it, is easy to interpret. Differentiating the second-order equation with respect to log S we obtain,

$$\frac{\mathrm{d}g}{\mathrm{d}(\log S)} = S\frac{\mathrm{d}g}{\mathrm{d}S} = c + 2d \log S. \tag{10}$$

This will, of course, be a straight line when plotted on semilog paper, on which S is measured along the horizontal axis and $S\mathrm{d}g/\mathrm{d}S$ along the vertical axis. The line will be positively inclined if the original curve was **U**-shaped upwards, i.e. if d is positive, and negatively inclined if the original curve was **U**-shaped downwards, i.e. if d is negative. In either case it will cross the horizontal axis at the turning point of the original curve. Both cases are illustrated in Figs. 1(a) and 1(b).

A straightforward interpretation can be given to $S\,dg/ds$, which we shall, from now on, refer to as Z. Rewriting Z as $dg/(dS/S)$, we see that it relates the *absolute* difference in g to the *proportionate* difference in S. That is, it shows how the relationship between growth and size changes with a change in size. For any small ΔS the resulting Δg will be given, approximately, by the following equation:

$$\Delta g = \frac{\Delta S}{S} \cdot S \frac{dg}{dS} = Z \cdot \frac{\Delta S}{S}. \tag{11}$$

It is important to note that Z differs from the *elasticity,* which relates the *proportionate* difference in g to the *proportionate* difference in S. Thus:

$$Z = s \frac{dg}{dS} = g \cdot \frac{S}{g}\frac{dg}{dS} = g \cdot \text{elasticity} \tag{12}$$

Whereas elasticity is a pure number, Z is measured in the same units as g. As g is measured in per cent per annum, so is Z.

Since the curve $Z = c + 2d \log S$ is a straight line relating Z to $\log S$, it is only necessary to determine two points on it in order to determine the entire curve. The most obvious points to determine are those corresponding to the smallest and largest firms in the relevant sample. Suppose the smallest and largest firms have opening sales of S_{min} and S_{max} respectively. The corresponding values of Z will be given by:

$$Z_{min} = c + 2d \log S_{min}, \tag{13}$$

$$Z_{max} = c + 2d \log S_{max}. \tag{14}$$

The value of Z, corresponding to any S lying between S_{min} and S_{max}, will lie between Z_{min} and Z_{max}.[4] Thus Z_{min} and Z_{max} define the outermost limits of Z for firms whose size lies within the range covered by the sample. It should be noted that Z_{min} need not be the minimum value of Z over the range of observations and Z_{max} need not be the maximum value. Only if d is positive will this be the case. If, on the other hand, d is negative then $Z_{min} \geqslant Z \geqslant Z_{max}$ for values of S between S_{min} and S_{max}, and Z_{min} will be the maximum value of Z and Z_{max} will be the minimum value.

Using the symbol '^' to denote an estimator, we can derive an estimator of any Z from the equation,

$$\hat{Z} = \hat{c} + 2\hat{d} \log S. \tag{15}$$

The estimator $\hat{Z}$ will have much the same properties as the original least squares estimators $\hat{c}$ and $\hat{d}$. Let us assume that the opening sizes of firms are fixed, known quantities. Then, provided the disturbances satisfy the condition $E(u) = 0$, the estimators $\hat{Z}$, $\hat{c}$, and $\hat{d}$ will all be unbiassed, i.e. $E(\hat{Z}) = Z$, $E(\hat{c}) = c$ and $E(\hat{d}) = d$. If the disturbances are independent of each other and have identical variances, i.e. $E(uu') = \sigma^2 I$, then $\hat{Z}$, $\hat{c}$, $\hat{d}$ will have variances at least as small as any other unbiassed linear estimators of Z, c and d.[5]

Finally, let $\hat{V}(\hat{c})$, $\hat{V}(\hat{d})$ and $\hat{\text{Cov}}(\hat{c}, \hat{d})$ denote the usual least squares estimators of variance and covariance. Suppose the variance of $\hat{Z}$ is estimated from the formula,

$$\hat{V}(\hat{Z}) = \hat{V}(\hat{c}) + 4 \log S \, \hat{\text{Cov}}(\hat{c}, d) + 4 \log^2 S \, \hat{V}(\hat{d}). \qquad (13)$$

Then if the disturbances are normally distributed, the variable $t = (\hat{Z} - Z)/\sqrt{[\hat{V}(\hat{Z})]}$ will have a t-distribution, with the appropriate degrees of freedom.

In particular if $Z_{min} = 0$ then $\hat{Z}_{min}/\sqrt{[\hat{V}(\hat{Z}_{min})]}$ has a t distribution, as has $\hat{Z}_{max}/\sqrt{[\hat{V}(\hat{Z}_{max})]}$ if $Z_{max} = 0$. Thus, if the disturbances are normally distributed, we can use a standard t test to test the hypotheses that $Z_{min} = 0$, or $Z_{max} = 0$.[6]

It is interesting to note from the hypothesis that *both* $Z_{min} = 0$ and $Z_{max} = 0$ is equivalent to the hypothesis that *both* $c = 0$ and $d = 0$. To test it does not, therefore, require the calculation of either $\hat{Z}_{min}$ or $\hat{Z}_{max}$.

When dealing with industry regressions we may obtain a number of values of $\hat{Z}_{min}$ or $\hat{Z}_{max}$ which seem to lie predominantly on one particular side of zero. It is useful to be able to apply a test which tells us whether or not this tendency is statistically significant. One such test is a variant of the χ^2 test which, for want of a better name, we shall call the α-test. A full description of the α-test is given in Appendix 2.

To illustrate its use let us consider a case in which we have a number of values of $\hat{Z}$ which seem to be predominantly negative. Assume, as a null hypothesis, that all 'true' values of Z are zero. On the basis of the null hypothesis, assuming the errors are normally distributed, we can construct a statistic α which is a function of the observed values of $\hat{Z}$ and of their estimated standard errors. If some of the observed values of $\hat{Z}$ are large and negative, α will be large and we shall reject the null hypothesis. If this happens we shall say that the $\hat{Z}$'s are *collectively significantly negative*. A slight variant of the test enables us to test whether or not there is a significant tendency for the Z's to be positive. If some of the Z's are large and positive we shall reject the null hypothesis and say that the $\hat{Z}$'s are *collectively significantly positive*. A collection of observed values can be both collectively significantly negative and collectively significant positive. This happens when there are a number of large negative values of $\hat{Z}$ and a number of large positive values. In other words, when the $\hat{Z}$'s are widely spread out on both sides of zero. If, on the other hand, collectively the $\hat{Z}$'s are neither significantly positive nor significantly negative then the bulk of them will be fairly close to zero.

4. Summary

We may summarise the basic method of analysis as follows. Growth, g, is assumed to be a function of size S given by the equation,

$$g = \text{constant} + \text{dummies} + c \log S + d \log^2 S + u,$$

where the dummies are variables whose value depends on the industry and country to which a firm belongs. Coefficients are estimated either by pooling firms from all countries and industries into one sample or by taking industries individually. Results are displayed in the form of estimates $\hat{Z}$ of $Z = dg/d(\log S)$. Because of the form of the equation chosen we shall have $\hat{Z} = \hat{c} + 2\hat{d} \log S$ where $\hat{c}$ and $\hat{d}$ are estimates of c and d. If S_{min} and S_{max} are the smallest and largest opening sizes in the particular sample we define $Z_{min} = c + 2d \log S_{min}$ and $Z_{max} = c + 2d \log S_{max}$. The corresponding estimates will be $\hat{Z}_{min}$ and $\hat{Z}_{max}$. For values of S within the range covered by the particular sample $\hat{Z}$ will lie between $\hat{Z}_{min}$ and $\hat{Z}_{max}$.

When d is positive $\hat{Z}_{max} \geqslant \hat{Z} \geqslant \hat{Z}_{min}$ and when d is negative $\hat{Z}_{max} \leqslant \hat{Z} \leqslant \hat{Z}_{min}$. To individual values of Z we can apply standard significance tests. To a collection of values of $\hat{Z}$ we can apply a variant of the χ^2 test, which we have called the α-test.

4. Size and growth

1. Introduction

In this chapter the relationship between size and growth is examined. First the performance of firms in the full and reduced samples during the years 1962–7 is compared; then the relationship between growth and size amongst firms of the full sample during 1962–7 is examined. On this basis the working hypothesis that, amongst small firms, growth was a decreasing function of size during 1962–7 and that, amongst large firms, these two variables were unrelated to each other is presented. In terms of the variables Z $(= dg/d(\log S))$ this hypothesis may be expressed as follows: Z was negative for small S and zero for large S.

A number of different tests are carried out to see how far the existence of specification errors and biasses may force the modification or even abandonment of our working hypothesis. Several samples are used, American and European firms are examined separately, and a third-order equation is tried instead of the original second-order equation. For American firms the hypothesis stands up fairly well. In the case of the Europeans, on the other hand, it seems that bias may account for some of the observed negative relationship between growth and size.

To conclude the chapter the relationship during the years 1957–62, and during the years 1957–67 as a whole is examined. Because of the restricted nature of the information available it is not possible to examine the relationship for firms other than those amongst the top 100 US and the top 100 non-US. Amongst these firms growth and size do not seem to be related to each other.

2. 1962–7

A working hypothesis

As a first step towards investigating the relationship between the size and rate of growth of firms during the years 1962–7, we may compare the performance of firms in our two samples – the reduced sample and the full sample. The full sample contains over 260 comparatively small firms which are not contained in the reduced sample. We should expect, therefore, any relationship between size and growth to be reflected as a difference between the average rates of growth of the firms in these two samples. If small firms grew slower than large firms then the full sample should yield a lower average.

Table 3 gives a selection of averages for the two samples.[1] In each of the six cases the firms of the full sample grew substantially faster than those of the reduced sample – by between 1 and 1½ per cent per annum. Thus small

Table 3 *Average growth rates of firms (% p.a.)*

	1962–7 adjusted		1962–7 unadjusted	
	Full sample	Reduced sample	Full sample	Reduced sample
USA	9.3	7.8	9.9	8.1
Europe	7.8	6.9	8.9	8.2
World	9.4	7.7	10.1	8.4

firms grew, on average, faster than large firms during 1962–7.

The same result can be obtained more formally by assuming some particular relationship between growth and size, and estimating its parameters. For the moment assume,

$$g = \text{constant} + \text{dummies} + c \log S + d \log^2 S + u. \tag{1}$$

Recall that differentiating Equation (1) we obtain:

$$Z = \frac{\mathrm{d}g}{\mathrm{d}(\log S)} = c + 2d \log S. \tag{2}$$

Where Z is positive g is an increasing function of S and where negative it is a decreasing function. If the smallest firm in a particular sample had opening sales of S_{min} and the largest has opening sales of S_{max}, we define Z_{min} and Z_{max} as the values of Z corresponding to S_{min} and S_{max} respectively. Their estimated values are denoted by $\hat{Z}_{min}$ and $\hat{Z}_{max}$.

Estimates based on the full sample of firms for 1962–7 are summarised in Table 4. (Complete results are given in Table 11 at the end of this chapter.)

Table 4 *Values of $\hat{Z}$ for the world, 1962–7. (Full sample.)*

Description		Industry (Proportion –ve)	Pooled (actual value)
$\hat{Z}_{min}$:	adjusted	8/9 (– **)	– 3.3 (– **)
	unadjusted	8/9 (–**)	–3.4 (– **)
$\hat{Z}_{max}$:	adjusted	5/9 (not sig.)	1.7 (not sig.)
	unadjusted	6/9 (not sig.)	0.1 (not sig.)

Significance. Collective significance of the industry $\hat{Z}$'s has been tested using a statistic α which, if the null hypothesis is correct, has a χ^2 distribution (see Appendix 2). The values of $\hat{Z}$, when firms from all industries are pooled together, have been tested using a *t*-test. In all cases the tests are one-tailed. Certain of these tests enable us to see whether a given value of $\hat{Z}$ or collection of such values is significantly negative. Others enable us to see whether they are significantly positive.

Significance is shown in parentheses. '–**', '–*', '–†' mean significantly negative at the 1, 5 and 10 per cent levels respectively. 'Not sig.' means significantly neither positive nor negative at the 10 per cent level.

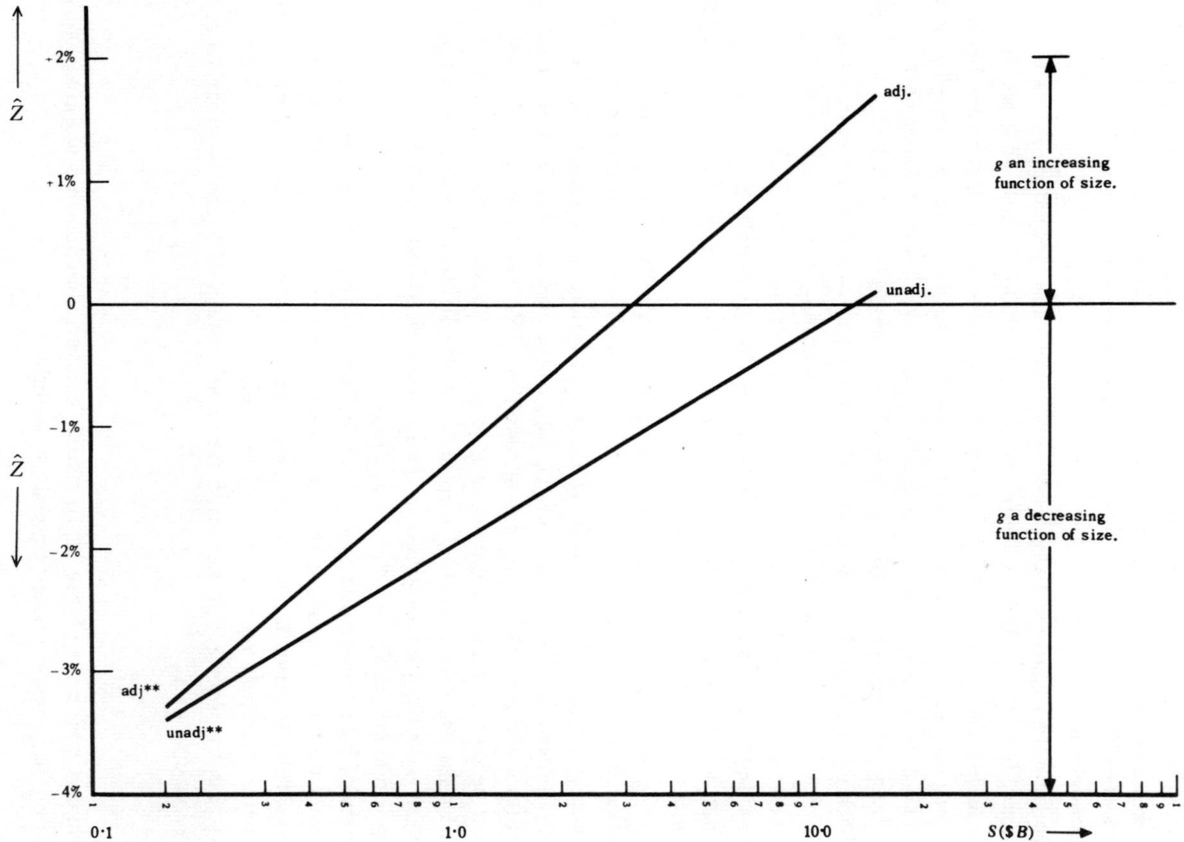

Fig. 2. $\hat{Z}$: all industries, 1962–7, world, full sample.

The first column shows the proportion of industries in which the relevant $\hat{Z}$ is negative. No collection of $\hat{Z}$'s in this or any other table shows a significant tendency to be positive. The second column shows the actual values of $\hat{Z}$ obtained when all firms are pooled into one sample and inter-industry differences are eliminated by means of dummies. In this table there are no significant positive values. Comparing the columns, we see that the industry regressions yield results broadly similar to those given by the 'pooled' regressions.

With either kind of data $\hat{Z}_{min}$ shows a pronounced tendency to be negative. In eight out of nine industries it is negative, and collectively these values are significantly negative at the 1 per cent level. The pooled $\hat{Z}_{min's}$ are are almost identical, being −3.3 per cent for adjusted data and −3.4 per cent for unadjusted data. These are significantly negative at the 1 per cent level.

When we turn to $\hat{Z}_{max}$ the two sets of results are not quite so close to each other. The differences, however, are not substantial. With adjusted data $\hat{Z}_{max}$ is negative in five out of nine industries and its pooled value is + 1.7 per cent. With unadjusted data there is a slightly greater tendency towards negative values, which are found in six out of nine industries. The pooled value is almost zero being equal to + 0.1 per cent. However, as none of the tests indicates any kind of significance, either positive or negative, we can conclude that both adjusted and unadjusted data lead to values of $\hat{Z}_{max}$ which are not significantly different from zero.

These results can most easily be interpreted visually. Fig. 2 portrays $\hat{Z}$ as a linear function of log S. Where a curve lies above the horizontal axis g is an increasing function of S and where it lies below the opposite is the case. It is clear that, over most of the range of sizes covered by the sample, our results show g to be a decreasing function of S. The curve for adjusted data lies below the axis for values of S less than $3,300 million. For unadjusted data the corresponding size is $13,000 million. These results are consistent with the picture given by Table 3 which shows small firms growing, on average, faster than large firms.

In view of this discussion, as a working hypothesis, assume that g is a decreasing function of size at the lower end of the scale, and that as size increases this relationship weakens until, amongst the very large firms, size and growth bear little or no relationship to each other. In terms of $\hat{Z}$, we may express this by saying $\hat{Z}$ is negative for small values of S and is close to zero for large values of S.

Specification and Bias.

The reasons which may force us to modify or even abandon this working hypothesis can be grouped under two main headings:

Specification. We have assumed that the relationship between g and S is correctly described by equation (1). This equation may, however, be inaccurate in two distinct ways. First, the relationship between g and S may vary from country to country. Amongst American firms, for example, the size coefficients or industry dummies may be radically different from their European equivalents. Secondly, even if the relationship is the same in each country, equation (1) may not be a correct expression of it. The true relationship may, for example, be best expressed by means of a third rather than second-order equation in log S. Alternatively, it may be the case that equation (1) is appropriate for the smaller firms in our sample but not for the larger firms. Finally, log S may not be the ideal size variable and some other, such as S, might have been better.

Bias. The choice of sample and treatment of data may be such as to cause serious biasses in the estimates of the parameters defining the relationship between g and S. These are summarised in Table 5.

Table 5 *Small-firm bias in growth rates*[1]

	US	Non-US	World
Full sample	0	++	+
Reduced sample	0	Not used[2]	0

1 A positive small-firm bias will usually make $\hat{Z}_{min}$ more negative and $\hat{Z}_{max}$ more positive.

2 The number of non-Americans in the reduced sample is too small to make its use worthwhile.

Bias is greatest when the non-American firms of the full sample are considered on their own. It is less when they are pooled with the Americans. When the non-Americans are excluded altogether and American firms are considered separately the bias is negligible. It is also negligible when the reduced sample is used instead of the full sample.

One problem remains. In checking whether there has been any specification error, we shall examine European firms separately. Since estimates based on the full sample of European firms are likely to be biassed, the natural course would be to use the reduced sample of European firms. Unfortunately this sample contains so few firms that the results would be extremely unreliable. We are forced, therefore, to rely upon biassed estimates when dealing with the Europeans. All we can do is make some rough guess at the likely magnitude and direction of this bias. This we do in Appendix 1. The effect of bias is to make Z_{min} appear more negative than it really is and Z_{max} more positive than it really is.

The next steps

To handle these problems we shall:

(1) Examine American and European firms separately. For the Americans this will both check for specification error and give unbiassed estimates.

For the Europeans it will merely check for specification error.

(2) Use the reduced sample instead of the full sample. This will both check for specification error and give unbiassed estimates.

(3) Add an extra term in $\log^3 S$. This will check specification error.

The use of S as an alternative to $\log S$ as an explanatory variable is examined in Appendix 3. Log S proved marginally preferable and is used throughout the chapter. None of the conclusions would have been substantially altered if S had been used instead.

Results given in the remainder of this chapter are based on adjusted data; unadjusted data produced almost identical results.

Europe and the United States

The results obtained when European and American firms are considered separately are given in Table 6. They are broadly similar. In each case $\hat{Z}_{min}$ is significantly negative both for an industry and pooled results. The values of $\hat{Z}_{max}$ are different, but this reflects the smaller size of S_{max} for the European sample rather than any difference in the relationship. The similarity of the two relationships comes out clearly when we compare the entire curves relating $\hat{Z}$ to $\log S$. In Fig. 3 these curves have been drawn for values of S between S_{min} and S_{max}. The European curve does not extend as far to the right because the European value of S_{max} is less than the American. Both curves are close to the 'world' curve which shows the results when all firms, American and non-American, are considered together.

Table 6 *Values of Z for Europe and the US, 1962–7. (Full sample, adjusted data.)*

Description		Industry (proportion –ve)	Pooled (actual value)
$\hat{Z}_{min}$:	Europe	5/8 (–†)	– 3.5 (–*)
	US	7/9 (–**)	– 3.4 (–**)
	World	8/9 (–**)	– 3.3 (–**)
$\hat{Z}_{max}$:	Europe	6/8 (not sig.)	0.4 (not sig.)
	US	5/9 (not sig.)	1.8 (not sig.)
	World	5/9 (not sig.)	1.7 (not sig.)

Notes. See Table 4.

This similarity may be deceptive. Looking at the pooled values, Europe's $\hat{Z}_{min}$ is less significant than its American counterpart. It is, moreover, negatively biassed. A combination of random errors and negative bias may have converted a near zero true value Z_{min} into the negative estimate, – 3.5 per cent. At the other end of the scale $\hat{Z}_{max}$ is positively biassed.

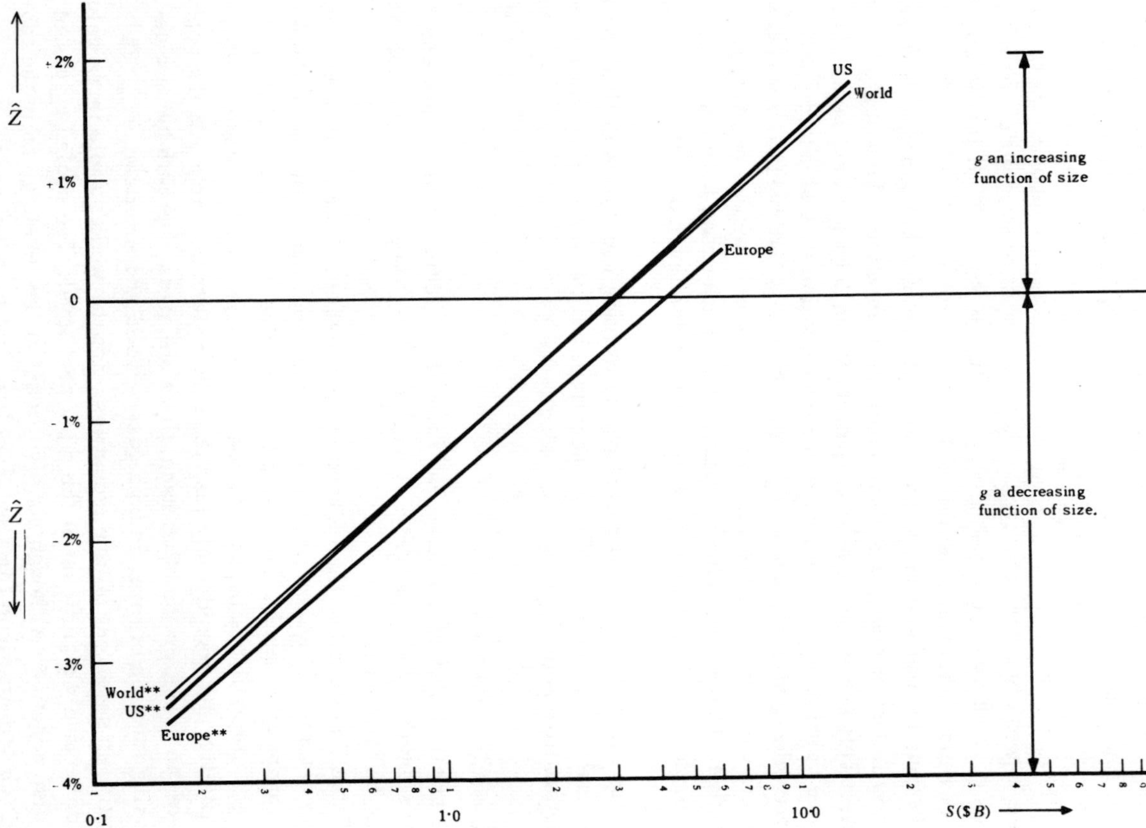

Fig. 3. $\hat{Z}$: all industries, 1962–7, full sample, adjusted data.

The true value Z_{max} may be negative. These suggestions are supported by the industry results. Only five out of eight European industries yield negative values of $\hat{Z}_{min}$, and collectively these are only significantly negative at the 10 per cent level. Six out of eight industries yield negative values of $\hat{Z}_{max}$, which are collectively not significantly positive or negative.

In view of the low significance of the $\hat{Z}$'s, the inconclusive industry results and the known biasses, it would be unwise to place much faith in the similarity of the European and American curves. The only fairly certain conclusion seems to be that $\hat{Z}$ is nowhere significantly, or even substantially, positive. There are, therefore, no signs of g being an increasing function of S. On the contrary, there is weak evidence to suggest that, over most or even all of the range of sizes covered by our sample, $\hat{Z}$ may be slightly negative. If this is so g will be a mildly decreasing function of S.

Turning to American firms, we find evidence of $\hat{Z}$ being negative when S is small. Out of nine industries, seven have negative values of $\hat{Z}_{min}$, and collectively these are significantly negative at the 1 per cent level. The pooled value of $\hat{Z}_{min}$ is negative and over six times its standard error. At the other end of the scale, $\hat{Z}_{min}$ is negative in five industries and positive in four. Collectively these values are significantly neither positive nor negative. The pooled value is positive but smaller than its standard error and is not, therefore, significantly different from zero even at the 25 per cent level.

Thus the American results confirm the working hypothesis of this section. For small values of S the $\hat{Z}$'s are negative, and for large S they are not very different from zero.

The reduced sample

The small number of non-American firms in the reduced sample prevented us from studying them separately. It was possible, however, to study the American firms on their own.

Table 7 summarises the reduced sample results. They are different from those obtained with the full sample. At the lower end of the scale there does not appear to be much relationship between size and growth. Industry values of $\hat{Z}_{min}$ are neither significantly positive or negative. The pooled values are positive but considerably less than their standard errors. At the upper end of the scale, on the other hand, there are signs of growth being a decreasing function of size. In both cases, world and American, $\hat{Z}_{max}$ is negative in seven out of nine industries. For the world sample these values are collectively significant at the 5 per cent level. The pooled values of $\hat{Z}_{max}$ are also negative. Although not significant at the levels given in the table, $\hat{Z}_{max}$ for the American firms is -1.24 times its standard error.

Table 7 *Values of $\hat{Z}$ for the world, 1962–7. (Adjusted data.)*

Description	Industry (proportion –ve)	Pooled (actual value)
$\hat{Z}_{min}$: world	3/9 (not sig.)	0.3 (not sig.)
US	4/9 (not sig.)	1.9 (not sig.)
$\hat{Z}_{max}$ world	7/9 (– *)	– 1.8 (not sig.)
US	7/9 (not sig.)	– 4.6 (not sig.)

Notes. See Table 4.

A third-order equation

The full sample results, confirmed for the US by a breakdown into two areas, suggest that g is a decreasing function of S for small values of S. The reduced sample results suggest that, for S in the middle range, there is little relationship between the two variables and that, for large S, g is once again a decreasing function of S.

This might suggest that the relationship between g and log S is best expressed not by a second-order equation but by some higher-order equation. To test this hypothesis let us add a term in $\log^3 S$, and estimate parameters of this new third-order equation using the full sample of adjusted data. Pooling all industries together and measuring S in hundreds of thousands of dollars, we obtain,

$$g = \text{constant} + \text{dummies} - \underset{(-1.91)}{107.23 \log S} + \underset{(1.80)}{11.09 \log^2 S} - \underset{(-1.71)}{0.38 \log^3 S} \tag{3}$$

$$R^2 = 0.260.$$

The terms in brackets are t-values denoting the ratio of coefficiencies to their standard errors.

Differentiating (3) with respect to log S, we obtain

$$\hat{Z} = -107.23 + 22.18 \log S - 1.14 \log^2 S \tag{4}$$

which is never positive, although it comes quite close to zero when sales are around one and a half billion dollars.

For small S, from Table 8, we see that the full sample second-order and third-order equations lead to similar values of $\hat{Z}$. For large S, on the other hand, the third-order results are closer to the second-order results based on the reduced sample.

In the middle range the third-order equation gives values of $\hat{Z}$ which are close to zero. Between \$500 million and \$5,000 million, for example, g is a uniformly decreasing function of S and yet the value of g at \$5,000 million is only about 1 per cent a year less than at \$500 million. An examination of the residuals suggests that in this range the third-order curve gives a fairly accurate picture of the relationship between g and S. When we look at the residuals for the very largest firms, those above \$5,000 million we find that the third-order curve overstates the degree to which growth diminishes with size.

Table 8 *Values of $\hat{Z}$ for the world, 1962–7. (Adjusted data.)*

Description	Pooled (actual value)	
	$\hat{Z}_{min}$	$\hat{Z}_{max}$
Full sample:		
Second-order equation	– 3.3 (–**)	1.7 (not sig.)
Third-order equation	– 3.3 (–**)	–5.8 (not sig.)
Reduced Sample:		
Second-order equation	0.3 (not sig.)	–1.8 (not sig.)

Notes. See Table 4.

Summary of results for 1962–7

The results for 1962–7 may be summed up by means of the diagram in Fig. 4. It is not drawn to scale.

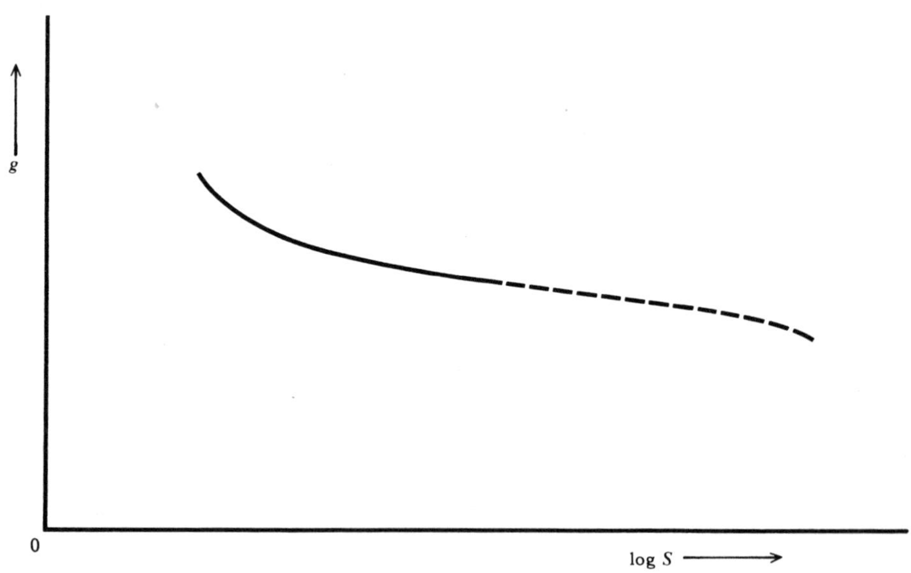

Fig. 4. g as a function of log S.

The height of the curve above the horizontal axis depends on the value of the dummies. The solid part of the line indicates that the results are fairly reliable, at least in the case of American firms. In the case of Europeans the results are less reliable as they are distorted by biasses of uncertain magnitude. The broken part of the line indicates the relationship most favoured by rather weak evidence.

3. 1957–62 and 1957–67

1957–62

The major difficulty when comparing the results just obtained with those of the earlier period 1957–62, arises from the restricted sample available for the earlier years. The negative relationship between g and S during 1962–7 was strongest amongst the bottom 200–300 firms, most of which are excluded from the reduced sample. Thus, even if a negative relationship for those firms had existed during 1957–62, it could not be observed with the restricted sample. However, the results derived from the reduced sample are of interest in their own right. Covering roughly the 200 biggest firms in the world, this sample includes a significant proportion of the firms with actual or potential world-wide operations. From Table 9 it can be seen that there is some difference between the results for 1957–62 and those obtained with the reduced sample for 1962–7. When all industries are pooled, the values of $\hat{Z}_{min}$ are 0.3 per cent and –4.5 per cent for 1962–7 and 1957–62 respectively. The latter is significantly different from zero at the 5 per cent level. The corresponding values of $\hat{Z}_{max}$ are – 1.8 per cent and 1.6 per cent respectively, neither of which is significantly different from zero.

Table 9 *Values of $\hat{Z}$ for the world. (Reduced sample, adjusted data)*

Description		Industry (proportion –ve)	Pooled (actual value)
$\hat{Z}_{min}$:	1957–62	4/9 (not sig.)	–4.5 (–*)
	1962–7	3/9 (not sig.)	0.3 (not sig.)
	1957–67	5/9 (not sig.)	–2.2 (–**)
$\hat{Z}_{max}$:	1957–62	6/9 (not sig.)	1.6 (not sig.)
	1962–7	7/9 (– *)	–1.8 (not sig.)
	1957–67	5/9 (not sig.)	0.4 (not sig.)

Notes. See Table 4.

It is interesting to note that there is a conflict between the results of industry and pooled regressions for 1957–62. Where the pooled regression gives a significantly negative value of $\hat{Z}_{min}$, some five out of nine industries have positive values. Collectively these values are significantly neither positive nor negative. Turning to $\hat{Z}_{max}$, we see that the pooled value is positive, whereas six out of nine industries have negative values.

If we apply an F-test to the pooled regression, we find that size is a significant explanatory variable at the 1 per cent level.[2] Even so, in view of the conflict between industry and pooled regressions, it would be unwise to accept any kind of relationship between g and S as being established. There is certainly no clear sign of a positive relationship between the two variables, and what signs there are of a negative relationship are not very convincing.

1957–67

Let us compare the results obtained for each of the two periods, industry by industry. Using the reduced sample of adjusted data, there appears to be very little continuity from one period to the next. From columns (7) and (8) of Table 10, it can be seen that not a single $\hat{Z}_{min}$ or $\hat{Z}_{max}$ is significantly different from zero in both periods. When the set of values of $\hat{Z}_{min}$ in each period are ranked according to their magnitude, there is little if any correlation between the two rankings.[3] Similarly the ranking of the two sets of values of $\hat{Z}_{max}$ are uncorrelated. Even when we look only at the significance of size as an explanatory variable, ignoring completely the signs and magnitudes of the coefficients, there is no continuity. If the F-values of Table 10, columns (7) and (8), are ranked according to size, there is little correlation between the two rankings.[4]

This lack of continuity is reflected in the results based on growth rates over the entire ten-year period 1957–67, which can be viewed as averages of the results obtained for the two five-year sub-periods. Significance levels are low and the various size effects, being averages of the effects in two periods, are fairly evenly scattered around zero. In one industry, food, size is a significant explanatory variable at the 5 per cent level, but in all others it fails to be significant even at the 25 per cent level. The only significant relationship comes from the pooled regression. The value of $\hat{Z}_{min}$ is equal to -2.2 per cent and is significant at the 1 per cent level. As this result is not confirmed by the industry regressions, it cannot be taken as convincing evidence of a relationship between g and S.

Our conclusions for the ten-year period 1957–67 must, therefore, be even more agnostic than those for either of the five-year sub-periods. Once again there is no sign that g is an increasing function of S, and once again there are signs that g may be a decreasing function of S for some values of S. As a glance at Table 11 shows, however, the industry $\hat{Z}$'s are so scattered that it would be unjustified to claim that any kind of relationship, positive or negative, exists between g and S.

4. Summary

With the data at our disposal this is about as far as we can go. To arrive at more definite conclusions we should need information about more firms, or else a greater number of time periods.

Amongst the smaller American firms, with sales in the region of $150 –

Table 10 *The significance of size: F values*

	(1)	(2)	(3)	(4)	(5)	(6)	(7)	(8)	(9)	(10)
	1962–7, full sample, adjusted data			1962–7, full sample, unadjusted data			Reduced sample, adjusted data			
Industry	US	Europe	World[1]	US	Europe	World[1]	1962–7 World[1]	1957–62 World[1]	1957–67 World[1]	1962–7 US
Food	0.77	2.96†	0.75	0.70	1.15	0.64	3.37††	2.54†	4.03*	2.35†
Chemicals	3.53*	0.23	3.90*	3.33*	0.70	4.25*	1.07	0.69	0.53	0.46
Oil	6.44**	0.02	5.80*	5.73*	0.02	6.16**	0.52	0.53	0.43	0.33
Iron and steel	0.38	3.46††	1.53	0.38	0.50	0.55	1.85†	1.22	1.00	0.52
Non-ferrous	4.31*	n.a.[2]	4.77*	4.29*	n.a.[2]	4.30*	2.61†	0.04	1.90	1.34
Engineering (ex. electrical)	3.68*	2.04†	1.15	0.53	1.26	0.98	3.61††	1.87†	1.32	2.37†
Electrical	2.38†	0.07	2.92††	1.52†	0.26	2.34†	0.11	2.85††	1.34	0.09
Autos	0.32	0.48	0.20	0.38	2.36†	0.69	0.99	0.28	0.39	0.86
Miscellaneous	0.23	5.25*	1.44†	0.37	4.87*	1.62†	1.74†	3.38*	0.56	1.58
All Industries	8.62	4.49*	13.45**	9.58**	5.73**	15.02**	0.71	6.86**	4.65*	1.18

[1] For individual industries US, Europe (inc. UK), and Japan only.

[2] More variables in the regression than observations.

Significance. *F*-test: ** = significant at 1% level; * = significant at 5% level; †† = significant at 10% level;
† = significant at 25% level.

Table 11 $\hat{Z}_{min}$ and $\hat{Z}_{max}$.

$\hat{Z}_{min}$ (% p.a.)

	(1)	(2)	(3)	(4)	(5)	(6)	(7)	(8)	(9)	(10)
	1962–7, full sample, adjusted data			1962–7, full sample, unadjusted data				Reduced sample, adjusted data		
Industry	US	Europe	World[1]	US	Europe	World[1]	1962–7 World[1]	1957–62 World[1]	1957–67 World[1]	1962–7 US
Food	1.0	−18.9*	0.5	−1.2	−15.3	−0.7	8.5	−4.2	−0.3	−2.1
Chemicals	−7.8*	−0.0	−5.4*	−7.6†	−7.4	−7.9**	2.3	4.9	2.9	−7.1
Oil	−9.4**	−2.8	−8.9**	−11.2**	−2.8	−11.0**	1.9	1.2	1.3	1.5
Iron and steel	−0.2	−18.3**	−3.7	−0.2	−10.1	−1.9	−6.4*	3.4	−1.4	0.3
Non-ferrous	−12.9†	n.a.[2]	−13.2†	−21.4*	n.a.[2]	−21.8*	−39.4*	−1.0	−26.7†	−47.1†
Engineering (ex. electrical)	−1.2	11.9	−0.4	−1.6	16.4	4.4	−10.1†	−5.5	−7.1	−9.8
Electrical	−3.8	1.7	−3.1†	−2.5	1.8	−2.4	2.4	7.0†	4.4	3.6
Autos	−3.3	7.0	−0.6	−2.4	−5.9	−1.5	3.1	0.7	1.4	12.8
Miscellaneous	0.7	6.7	−1.1	−0.9	−6.6	−2.2	17.1*	−14.6	−6.6	18.8*
All Industries	−3.4**	−3.5*	−3.3**	−3.1**	−5.2	−3.4**	0.3	−4.5**	−2.2**	1.9

Table 11 continued

Z_{max} (% p.a.)

	(1)	(2)	(3)	(4)	(5)	(6)	(7)	(8)	(9)	(10)
	1962–7, full sample, adjusted data			1962–7, full sample, unadjusted data			Reduced sample, adjusted data			
Industry	US	Europe	World[1]	US	Europe	World[1]	1962–7 World[1]	1957–62 World[1]	1957–67 World[1]	1962–7 US
Food	–3.6	52.8*	–3.0	–2.0	50.0	–2.1	–11.7**	–1.8	–5.3†	–6.0
Chemicals	2.6	–2.6	2.0	1.6	3.7	3.8	–7.5	–1.3	–3.7	1.9
Oil	5.9**	–0.8	5.2*	3.2	–0.8	3.0	–1.4	0.3	–0.4	–0.8
Iron and steel	–1.7	12.6*	1.5	–1.7	6.6	–0.1	2.7	–5.4†	–1.6	–1.9
Non-ferrous	–0.9	n.a.[2]	–0.9	8.6	n.a.[2]	8.3	44.6†	–0.6	17.3	36.0
Engineering (ex. electrical)	–2.6	23.2†	–4.7	–5.6	–24.2	–9.1	–2.3	10.0*	0.6	–0.7
Electrical	0.7	–2.0	0.4	–0.8	–3.7	–0.8	–3.1	–9.1**	–7.0†	–4.4
Autos	1.9	–9.2	–0.7	0.1	–4.7	–1.1	–6.3	3.2	0.1	–16.3
Miscellaneous	–2.3	–3.8	–2.6	–1.4	–3.9	–1.8	–11.0†	–1.2	1.8	–11.6†
all industries	1.8	0.4	1.7	–0.1	0.7	0.1	–1.8	1.6	0.4	–4.6

Notes: See Table 10.

Definitions. $Z_{min} = S dg/dS$ (evaluated at $S = S_{min}$), $Z_{max} = S dg/dS$ (evaluated at $S = S_{max}$).

Significance: Two tailed *t*-test: ** = significant at the 5% level; * = significant at the 10% level; † = significant at the 20% level.

$500 million a year, growth seems to have been a decreasing function of size during 1962–7. There might have been a similar relationship amongst the non-American firms, but this is not certain in view of the ineradicable biasses in the data. For the earlier time period, it was impossible to examine the relationship amongst smaller firms as most of them were not in the reduced sample. Amongst medium and large firms there are signs that in each period growth was a decreasing function of size. The evidence, however, is weak.

One conclusion stands out clearly from all this. Growth was not an increasing function of size. Big firms did not grow faster than small firms. On the contrary, during 1962–7 firms which were small by international standards, grew faster than the giants. Apart from this, size and growth seem to have been largely independent of each other.

5. Nationality and growth

1. Introduction

When discussing the effect of size on growth, in the previous chapter, industry and nationality effects were not discussed explicitly, although they were controlled by means of dummy variables. In this chapter we shall consider the effects of nationality as indicated by the coefficients of certain dummy variables in regression equations similar to those used in the previous chapter. These are the estimated values of the a's in equations of the general form,

$$g = e + \sum_{i=2}^{m} a_i C_i + \sum_{j=1}^{n-1} b_j I_j + u$$

when industries are pooled together. When dealing with individual industries this becomes

$$g_j = e_j + a_{j\,\mathrm{UK}} C_{\mathrm{UK}} + a_{j\,\mathrm{Eu}} C_{\mathrm{Eu}} + a_{j\,\mathrm{Ja}} C_{\mathrm{Ja}} + u_j$$

for the jth industry. The C's and the I's are dummy variables which take the value 1 for a firm in the appropriate country or industry and 0 otherwise.

The chapter begins by examining estimates based on adjusted data for the periods 1957–62, 1962–7 and 1957–67. No explicit attempt is made to allow for the influence of size on growth, although the use of two different samples makes some implicit allowance. Bias in the full sample estimates for 1962–7 is corrected by the use of a modified version of this sample. Next, the chapter examines the extent to which estimates depend on the treatment of biasses, the choice of sample, whether or not the data are adjusted, and whether or not the influence of size is removed. Because sales are measured in current US dollars it is possible that parts of the estimated differences in growth rates are due to different rates of domestic inflation. The chapter is concluded, therefore, by an examination of the impact of inflation on growth rates. The growth of a firm is taken throughout to be the growth of its total sales, including those produced by overseas subsidiaries.

2. International differences

1957–62

It can be seen from Table 12 that during the years 1957–62 the gap between the growth rates of American firms, on the one hand, and Japanese and

D

Table 12 *Average growth rate of firms. (% p.a. adjusted data)*

	Full Sample	Reduced Sample		
	1962–7	1962–7	1957–62	1957–67
USA	9.3	7.8	3.1	5.4
Germany	5.8	5.5	10.5	7.9
France	7.9	7.0	8.4	7.7
Benelux	7.9	8.1	8.6	8.3
Italy	8.9	10.4	14.9	12.5
UK	8.1	6.5	3.0	4.7
Other EFTA	10.3	9.0	9.8	9.4
Japan	16.4	17.1	12.4	14.7
Canada	9.7	10.3	2.5	6.4
Other	10.0	13.7	6.8	10.2
All	9.4	7.7	4.7	6.2
Non-US	9.6	7.7	6.8	7.2
Europe	7.8	6.9	6.9	6.8
Continental Europe	7.6	7.1	10.0	8.5
EEC	7.1	6.8	10.1	8.4

Table 13 *International differences. (All industries pooled) (% p.a.)*

	Full Sample,	Reduced Sample,		
	1962–7 (unbiassed)	1962–7	1957–62	1957–67
	(1)	(2)	(3)	(4)
UK–US	–1.5†	–1.2	–0.3	–0.7
Germany–US	–4.5**	–2.3††	7.6**	2.7**
France–US	–2.2†	–0.4	5.3**	2.5*
Benelux	–1.9	0.8	6.9**	3.8*
Italy–US	–1.3	1.6	10.2**	5.9**
Other EFTA–US	–0.5	0.1	5.2**	2.7*
Japan	6.2**	11.9*	12.1**	12.0**
Canada–US	–0.6	2.8	0.7	1.8
Other–US	–0.9	5.4†	4.2	4.7*

Notes. All estimates are derived from regressions based on adjusted data. No size variables were included.

The differences (UK – US), etc. are the estimated values of the a_i's in

$$g = e + \sum_{i=2}^{m} a_i C_i + \sum_{j=1}^{n-1} b_j I_j + u$$

Significance. Two tailed *t*-test: ** = 1% level; * = 5% level; †† = 10% level; † = 20% level.

Continental Europeans, on the other, was enormous. In the two industries in which Japan was represented her firms grew by an average of 12 per cent a year faster than their American equivalents. Continental European firms grew, on average, faster than the American firms in every one of the eight industries in which they were represented. In four of these industries the differences were statistically significant at the 1 per cent level.

From the results of the pooled regressions given in Table 13 it can be seen that the overall differences were positive and significant for everyone of the continental European countries. Slowest were the continental EFTA firms which averaged 5.2 per ce nt a year more that the American firms and fastest were the Italian firms which averaged 10.2 per cent a year more.

Table 14 *Proportion of industries with positive differences*

	Full sample 1962–7 (Unbiassed)	Reduced sample, 1962–7	1957–62	1957–67
UK – US	2/9 (–*)	3/8 (not sig.)	4/8 (– †)	3/8 (not sig)
Continental EU – US	2/9 (–**)	3/8 (not sig.)	8/8 (+**)	7/8 (+**)
Japan – US	7/8 (+**)	2/2 (+**)	2/2 (+**)	2/2 (+**)

Notes. All data is adjusted. No size variables were included in the regressions. A positive difference occurs in an industry when the firms of the relevant country grow faster than the American firms.

For the jth industry the differences (UK – US), etc. are the estimated values of the a's in:

$$g_j = e_j + a_{j\,\mathrm{UK}} C_{\mathrm{UK}} + a_{j\mathrm{EU}} C_{\mathrm{EU}} + a_{j\mathrm{Ja}} C_{\mathrm{Ja}} + u_j$$

Significance. Collective significance is shown in brackets, '+' indicates that the differences were positive, and '–' significantly negative. See Table 4 for the meaning of other symbols.

The experience of the Anglo-Saxon countries – Britain and Canada – was radically different from that of the other non-Americans. In most industries British firms grew at much the same rate as American firms. The exceptions were oil, where American firms grew significantly faster, and engineering, where they grew significantly slower. To see if these industry differences were collectively significant, an α-test was used. This indicated that British firms grew, on balance, a little slower than those of the United States. The evidence for this conclusion is, however, weak. The α value was only significant at the 10 per cent level. Moreover, when all industries are pooled the difference between British and American firms has the small and statistically insignificant value of –0.3 per cent a year.

In conclusion, therefore, the performances of the firms of the two countries were rather similar, and the American firms had at most a slight edge over the British.

The Canadian firms did a little better than the British and managed to grow faster than the American firms by an average of 0.7 per cent a year. The difference, however, was statistically insignificant.

The experience of the years 1957–62 may be summed up as follows. The leaders were the Japanese who were followed by the Continental Europeans. Well behind them, bunched fairly closely together, came the Canadians, and finally the British. These conclusions are summarised in Table 14 which gives the proportion of industries where the firms of the major 'countries' grew faster than the Americans. It also gives the collective significance of the industry differences.

1962–7

During 1962–7 Japanese firms continued to grow much faster than American. Average growth rates for the full sample were greater than those of American firms in seven out of eight industries, and the α-test shows that, collectively, the differences were significant at the 1 per cent level. When all industries are pooled the average Japanese firm grows at 6.2 per cent a year faster than the average American firm, a figure which is statistically significant at the 1 per cent level.

The gap between Japanese and American growth rates becomes even greater when the full sample is replaced by the reduced sample. This is not, however, due to a difference in the relative performance of Japanese firms in the two samples, but to the different industrial composition of the two groups of Japanese firms. The Japanese firms of the reduced sample came entirely from engineering and iron and steel, two industries in which the Japanese have done particularly well. When the full sample is used, however, a number of Japanese firms from other industries enter and the Japanese performance, although still much better than that of other countries, looks a little less spectacular.

Continental European firms, by contrast, were unable to maintain their lead over American firms. After allowing for bias, the average growth rate of the continentals in the full sample was less than that of the Americans in seven out of nine industries (see Table 14). An α-test indicated that, collectively, these differences were significantly negative at the 1 per cent level, a result confirmed by the pooled regression which gave negative differences for every continental European country (see Table 13). Most striking were the low growth rates of German and French firms, which lagged behind the Americans by an average of 4.5 per cent and 2.2 per cent a year, respectively.

The results derived from the reduced sample, on the other hand, create a less distinct impression. The firms of three continental European countries grew faster than those of the United States and those of two grew more slowly. None of the differences is very significant (see Table 13). In three industries the Continentals grew faster than the Americans and in five they grew more slowly. Collectively the differences were not significant even at the 25 per cent level (see Table 14).

Turning to the UK, there is a rather similar picture. Amongst the firms of the full sample, the Americans do rather better than the British, although the difference is not as great as in the case of the Continentals. Once again the American performance is not as good when the full sample is replaced by the reduced sample. In three industries British firms grew faster and in five they grew more slowly. Collectively these industry differences were only just significantly negative at the 25% level. Moreover, when all industries are pooled, the difference between British and American firms of – 1.2 per cent a year is small and statistically insignificant.

Finally the performance of Canadian firms was similar to that of the Americans. On average the Canadians of the full sample grew by 0.6 per cent a year more slowly that the Americans and those of the reduced sample by 2.8 per cent more quickly. In neither case was the difference statistically significant.

Looking at individual industries we find that the Americans did particularly well in the electrical industry. Those in the full sample grew by between 4 and 7 per cent a year faster than the British or the continental Europeans. In every case the differences were statistically significant. Amongst the firms of the reduced sample the American lead was rather smaller and not usually statistically significant. Perhaps most striking was the ability of the American firms of the full sample to keep up with their Japanese rivals in the electrical industry. Indeed this was the only industry where they were able to do so. Non-electrical engineering was also an industry where the Americans had a substantial, if not so statistically significant, lead over the British and Continentals in 1962–7. Here, however, they were not able to keep up with the Japanese who grew at about 8 per cent a year faster. In other industries the American performance was less impressive and in no case did they have a clear lead.

The general picture to emerge shows Japanese firms well in the lead, followed by the Anglo-Saxons, and behind them the continental Europeans. As can be seen from Tables 19 and 20, the exact positioning of the non-Japanese firms, and the significance of the differences between them varies a little according to the method of estimation chosen. The main variation occurs when we change samples. The gap between the Americans, on one hand, and the Europeans, including the British, on the other, is much smaller when the reduced sample is used. Thus the very largest European firms, which make up the reduced sample, were more or less able to hold their own against the Americans, whereas the Europeans of the full sample fell a little behind.

An obvious but incorrect explanation is that this reflects the superior performance of big as compared to small European firms. But, as we know, this was not so. The smaller European firms appear to have grown a little faster than the bigger ones.

The true explanation is to be found, not in differences in performance between big and small European firms, but in differences between big and small American firms. For, as is shown in the previous chapter, growth was negatively related to size amongst American firms. The small American firms grew faster than the large. In switching from the reduced to the full sample, we bring in a number of these fast-growing American firms. As a result, the European firms, who previously seemed to be holding their own, are now outpaced by the Americans, particularly in the engineering and electrical industries.

A comparison

It is interesting to compare the results obtained, using the reduced sample, for each of the two periods. On the most general level it is clear from Tables 13, 14 and 15 that the really striking change in relative performance has been the dropping back of the Continental Europeans. Every one of these five 'countries' has dropped back relative to the Americans by between 5.1 per cent a year in the case of the continental EFTA countries to 9.9 per cent a year in the case of Germany (see Table 15). Confirmation is provided by Table 16, which gives an industrial breakdown of the changes in relative position. In seven out of eight industries the Continentals dropped back to amounts ranging from 5.4 per cent a year in chemicals to 14.4 per cent a year in autos. Only in oil did they just manage to hold their own.

Table 15 *Changes in relative performance 1957–62 to 1962–7.* *(By country)*

	% per annum
UK – US	– 0.9
Germany – US	– 9.9
France – US	– 5.7
Benelux – US	– 6.1
Italy	– 8.6
Other EFTA – US	– 5.1
Japan – US	– 0.2
Canada – US	+ 2.1

Source. These figures are derived from Table 13, by subtracting column (3) from column (2).

The change in the British position, on the other hand, was less clear cut. In four industries the relative performance of British firms improved and in four it became worse. Amongst those where it improved were food, chemicals and oil where British firms are known to be strong. Amongst those where it became worse were engineering, electricals and autos.

Turning to the industrial pattern of American recovery, we see no clear tendency for any coherent group of industries to be responsible. It is clear from Table 16, that the improvement in the American performance has not been confined to the 'growth' or 'modern' industries. On the contrary, it seems to have occurred fairly randomly and affected most sectors. It is true that in 1962–7 American firms in the engineering and electrical industries were growing much faster than their continental equivalents. But this does not reflect a more than average improvement in these industries. It reflects, rather, a permanent American strength in engineering and electricals. In 1957–62 the American firms of these industries, although they grew more slowly, performed comparatively better against the Continentals than did the firms of most other industries.

Table 16 *Changes in relative performance 1957–62 to 1962–7. (By industry)*

	% per annum		
	UK–US	Continental Europe–US	Japan–US
Food	+2.2	–6.6	
Chemicals	+4.0	–5.4	
Oil	+5.7	+0.6	
Iron and steel	–2.7	–8.2	–0.8
Non-ferrous			
Engineering (ex. electrical)	–11.4	–7.9	–2.5
Electrical	–5.7	–7.4	
Autos	–6.9	–14.9	
Miscellaneous	+1.4	–13.4	

Source. These figures are derived from Table 19 by subtracting row 11 from row 7.

1957–67

Although American and British firms made something of a come-back in the second period, this was nothing like enough to compensate for their slow growth in the earlier years. Over the ten years 1957–67 as a whole the continental Europeans grew faster than the Americans in seven out of eight industries. Only in engineering did the Americans hold their own. Moreover, the firms of every continental country grew faster than those of the United States (see Table 13).

British firms, on the other hand, grew at much the same rate as the Americans over the decade. In only one industry, oil, was the difference between British and American growth rates significantly different from zero at the 20 per cent level.

Over the ten years 1957–67, therefore, the leader was Japan followed by continental Europe. Well behind came the closely bunched Anglo-Saxons : Canada, the US, and finally the UK.

3. Problems of estimation

To find out how far the results depended on the exact method of estimation chosen, various approaches were tried. Altogether, for the years 1962–7 ten methods were employed for each industry and the same number for all industries combined. For 1957–62 and 1957–67, on the other hand, it was only necessary to use two methods for each industry and for all industries combined.

The resulting estimates, which are given in full in Table 19 and 20 at the end of the chapter, are surprisingly close to each other. In any particular industry or when all industries are combined, the estimates do not seem to depend very much on which method of estimation is chosen . What variations there are can be conveniently summarised under three headings : bias, adjustment, and sample.

Bias. The method used to estimate the relationship between size and growth, for the firms of the full sample in 1962–7 introduced an *upward* bias in the estimated growth rate of non-American firms. As explained in Chapter 2 this can be eliminated by dropping the small slow-growing American firms which failed to appear in the top 300 in 1967.

Comparing the 'unbiassed' estimates with their biassed equivalents, we see that the relative performance of American firms at the industry level improves by anything up to 1 per cent a year when bias is removed. For the average industry, however, the change is fairly small, amounting to an improvement of something like half a percent a year.

Adjustment. The main effect of adjustment is to remove the excessively high growth rates caused by mergers. Accordingly, those countries whose firms took part in mergers large enough to be removed by our adjustments do rather less well after adjustment than those for which mergers were not important. In the oil industry, for example, adjustment lowers the relative performance of American firms by around 3 per cent a year. In other industries, however, American firms seem to have merged rather less than those of other countries. Moreover, the Americans gain from the allowance made in adjusted data for the US copper strike in 1967. On balance the effect of adjustment is not very large. Relative to French and Italian firms the American performance improves noticeably. Otherwise the change is small, usually less than half a percent a year.

Sample. It was shown in the previous chapter that size was not a very important determinant of growth. Only in the case of American firms in 1962–7 was there clear evidence of size being related to growth. This is reflected in the superior relative performance of American firms of the full sample as compared to that of American firms of the reduced sample. Otherwise, estimates of international differences do not alter very much when size variables are included in the regressions.

The final choice

The above discussion suggests that the most crucial question was which sample to use. Rather than prejudge the issue both samples were used.

The other decisions do not appear so crucial, and the broad picture does not depend on whether or not the bias is removed, whether or not the data is adjusted, or even whether or not size is included as an explanatory variable. We were, therefore, free to make these decisions on the basis of convenience rather than theoretical exactness. From the point of view of convenience it is obviously better to exclude size variables, for then the industry regressions yield coefficients which are equal to differences in *average* growth rates. Such differences have an immediate intuitive meaning. From a theoretical point of view it is better to rely upon 'unbiassed' estimates when dealing with the full sample. The results in the text were based, therefore, on both the full and the reduced samples. Estimates were derived from regressions in which no size variables had been included. Data were adjusted, and the full sample estimates were 'unbiassed'.

4. Volumes and values

Inflation

The results presented above are open to a potentially serious objection. Growth rates have been derived from sales measured at current prices, converted to US dollars at official exchange rates. Provided these exchange rates behave so as to offset exactly differential rates of price inflation, international differences in the rates of growth of sales, measured in current US dollars, will exactly equal differences in rates of growth of sales measured by volume. As a general rule, however, exchange rates will not behave in this way. Official exchange rates are subject to a wide variety of influences and may not vary so as to maintain 'purchasing power parity'. Sales, measured in dollars, of any firm selling a large proportion of its goods in a country with a high rate of inflation uncompensated by exchange rate adjustment, will tend to grow faster than those of a firm selling mainly in another market where dollar prices are rising more slowly.

National price indices

If our estimates are to be taken as a guide to the relative performance of firms, when their sales are measured by volume, it is clear that some attempt must be made to assess the magnitude and importance of relative dollar price movements. The most obvious, indeed the only feasible, way of doing this is to construct for each country an index of the price in dollars of industrial products. Such an index will not, of course, be a perfect index of the prices of goods produced by the firms in our sample. For one thing, these firms may have a different product mix from the average, or their prices for a given product may behave differently from the average.

Even if national indices were a perfect guide to the price of goods sold by our firms in a particular national market, they might still be misleading. Many firms sell a substantial proportion of their output overseas and domestic prices may not be closely related to the prices at which they sell the goods they export or produce abroad. The appropriate index for such a firm would not be a single national index but rather a weighted sum of national indices. In the extreme case, where all firms in an entire sample sold the same proportion of their goods in each particular national market, these weights would be the same for all firms. The sales of every firm would then have the same price index and international differences in rates of growth of dollar and volume sales would be identical. Firms are not, however, equally 'international' in this sense and some allowance must be made for differential rates of dollar price inflation. The correct allowance will lie somewhere between zero, which corresponds to completely 'international' firms, and a figure based upon the assumption that all firms are completely 'national'.

The national indices used to eliminate the effects of inflation were derived from wholesale price indices given in the OECD publication *Main Economic Indicators*. Unfortunately, the coverage of the original series varied from country to country and did not always include manufacturing, mining and petroleum. From the data given, however, we were able to construct composite indices. Official exchange rates were used to convert these into dollar price indices. These were then expressed as the annual percentage rates of change given in Table 21.

Using these rates of change, the international differences in growth rates given in Table 13 can be corrected. The result is the set of 'real' differences given in Table 18. Before looking at these real differences, however, let us examine the rates of change of dollar prices in various countries. This will give us an idea of how large the distortions introduced by using values instead of volumes are likely to be.

Table 17 *Dollar prices relative to those of the US (Annual percentage changes)*

	1962–7	1957–62	1957–67
Continental Europe	0.7	0.4	0.5
UK	0.2	1.0	0.6
Japan	0.4	–0.4	–0.1
Canada	0.8	–0.8	0.0

Source. Table 21

Method. Let p_i and p_{US} be the rates of change of dollar prices in country i and in the US respectively. The rate of change of relative dollar prices is approximately equal to $p_i - p_{US}$.

From Table 17 it is clear that dollar prices behaved rather similarly to those of the US, particularly during 1962–7 and the longer period 1957–67. During 1962–7, for example, the highest rate of price change was less than 1 per cent a year greater than the lowest. In 1957–62, on the other hand, the differences were larger. British dollar prices rose by 1.8 per cent a year more than those of Canada. It must be remembered, however, that the British firms of the sample sold and produced a comparatively large proportion of their output overseas or in direct competition with foreign firms. As a result their prices probably rose by less than our index suggests. Even so, it is clear that in the early period prices were of some importance in determining relative growth rates. This becomes particularly clear when we look at individual continental countries.

Table 18 *International differences in 'real' growth rates. (All industries pooled)* (% p.a.)

	Full sample, 1962–7 (unbiassed)	Reduced sample, 1962–7	1957–62	1957–67
UK – US	–1.7	–1.4	–1.3	–1.3
Germany – US	–4.9	–2.7	5.6	1.5
France – US	–2.6	–0.8	6.7	3.0
Benelux	–3.5	–0.8	7.1	3.1
Italy – US	–2.1	0.8	10.8	5.8
Other EFTA – US	–2.5	–0.9	5.2	2.2
Japan – US	5.8	11.5	12.5	12.1
Canada – US	–1.4	2.0	1.5	1.8

Source. Tables 13 and 21.

Method: The differences (UK – US), etc. are the same as the a_j's in Table 13, adjusted to remove the effects of different rates of inflation.

The German revaluation of 1961 and the French devaluations of 1957 and 1958 did not exactly offset domestic price changes. German revaluation raised the dollar price of goods whose prices had already been rising faster than those of the Americans. French devaluation overcompensated for domestic inflation. As a result German dollar prices rose during 1957–62 by 2.6 per cent a year and French dollar prices fell by 0.8 per cent a year (see Table 21). It is interesting to note that this difference is enough to reverse the relative positions of French and German firms, when we look at volumes rather than values. At official exchange rates the sales of German firms rose during 1957–62 by 10.5 per cent a year and those of French firms by 8.4 per cent a year. By volume, on the other hand, the growth rates were 7.9 per cent a year and 9.2 per cent a year respectively. A German lead of 2.1 per cent a year in values becomes, therefore, a 1.3 percent a year lag in volumes. When these countries are pooled with the other continentals, however, extremes are set off against each other and the overall rate of change of Continental prices is not very different from that of the United States.

'Real' differences

Let us now return to Table 18. Its general features are very close to those of Table 13, a fact which is hardly surprising in view of the comparatively small relative price changes.

Japanese firms have, as before, a clear lead in each period. The Continentals grow considerable faster than the British, Americans, or Canadians during 1957–62. In 1962–7 there occurs the reversal we have observed in the case of values. Amongst the firms of the full sample the Continentals are unable to keep up with the Americans. The Americans' lead varies from 2.1 percent a year over the Italians to 4.9 percent a year over the Germans. Even the Continentals of the reduced sample fall a little behind. The British and the Canadians, by contrast, perform very much the same in each period. The British grow about 1½ percent a year more slowly than the Americans in each period, and the Canadians about 1½ per cent a year faster. This latter figure, however, is rather unreliable as it depends on the sample. When the full sample is used the Canadians grow more slowly.

In the movement from values to volumes, therefore, our conclusions have remained more or less intact. During 1962–7 the tendency of the Americans to pull ahead of the Continentals, and to a lesser extent of the British, has been reinforced. So too has the tendency of the British to fall behind during 1957–62. Otherwise the changes have been negligible.

5. Summary

The estimated effects of nationality on growth do not depend to any great extent on whether the data is adjusted, nor on whether allowance is made for different rates of domestic inflation, nor on whether an explicit allowance is made for the effects of size. They do, however, depend to some extent on which sample is used for the years 1962–7. When the full sample is used the Americans grow rather faster than when the reduced sample is used.

During 1957–62 the Japanese were leaders, followed by the Continental Europeans, and well behind them the closely bunched Anglo-Saxons – Canada, The United States, and Britain. In 1962–7 the Anglo-Saxons made something of a recovery and the order was Japan well in the lead again, followed by the Anglo-Saxons, and behind them the Continentals. The exact order during 1962–7 depends on the method of estimation. The main variation occurs when we change samples. The Continental 'giants' of the reduced sample were more or less able to hold their own against the American 'giants' of the reduced sample. When the full sample is used, however, and smaller firms are introduced, the Continentals do not do so well, for they are outpaced by the fast growing Americans of the top 100–300.

The American recovery from one period to the next does not seem to have followed any clear industrial pattern. In particular, it was not confined to the 'modern' industries, where one would expect to see the most visible signs of an American technological 'challenge'. The clear American lead over the British and Continentals in electricals and engineering during 1962–7 reflects a permanent strength in these fields rather than a particularly strong recovery.

The apparent 'challenge' of the American lead in electricals and engineering in 1962–7 must be put into perspective by looking both at their performance in other industries and in the earlier period 1957–62. In chemicals, oil, and autos, which may be considered other 'modern' industries, there was no clear American lead in 1962–7, and in some cases there were signs of a European lead. Moreover, even in electricals and engineering the Americans grew more slowly that the British and Continentals in 1957–62.

Over the ten years 1957–67 as a whole the clear leaders were the Japanese, followed by the continental Europeans, and some way behind them the Anglo-Saxons. The gap between the Continentals and the Americans varied from a German lead of 5.9 percent per annum to a French lead of 2.5 percent per annum. The Continentals grew faster than the Americans in seven out of eight industries.

Table 19 *International differences (by industry) (% p.a.) (UK–US)*

	Food	Chemicals	Oil	Iron and steel	non-ferrous	Engineering (ex. electrical)	Electrical	Autos	Miscellaneous	α-test
1962–7, Full sample										
Biassed										
1. Adj. without log *S*	3.0††	–1.3	–1.3	–1.1	14.6*	–7.0*	–6.5**	0.5	–0.5	–*
2. Adj. with log *S*	2.7††	0.1	0.5	–1.6	6.6	–6.1††	–6.6**	0.4	–0.4	–*
3. Unadj. without log *S*	3.5††	–1.8	–4.5	–1.1	20.4*	–7.6††	–4.6††	2.2	–1.3	–†
4. Unadj. with log *S*	3.2†	–0.3	0.0	–1.6	10.2†	–7.7††	–4.9*	2.1	–1.2	–†
Unbiassed										
5. Adj. without log *S*	2.2	–2.5	–1.4	–1.5	14.6*	–7.4*	–6.9**	0.0	–1.3	–*
6. Adj. with log *S*	1.1	–0.8	0.2	–2.5	6.6	–6.2††	–7.2	–0.2	–1.6	–*
1962–67, Reduced sample										
7. Adj. without log *S*	1.7	1.9	0.2	–0.5		–5.8†	–4.8†	–2.4	–1.8	–†
8. Adj. with log *S*	2.0	4.1	–0.2	–3.8†		–8.6*	–4.6	–4.8	–2.0	–*
9. Unadj. without log *S*	3.2†	1.9	–2.6	–0.5		–5.8†	–1.7	1.7	–2.4	not sig.
10. Unadj. with log *S*	5.0†	4.2	–0.2	–4.4		–8.6*	–1.9	–4.2	–2.8	–††
1957–62										
11. Adj. without log *S*	–0.5	–2.1	–5.5**	2.2		5.6*	0.9	4.5	–3.2	–††
12. Adj. with log *S*	–3.3†	–2.6	–6.4**	2.2		7.5*	1.4	8.7	–5.4††	–*
1957–67										
13. Adj. without log *S*	0.6	–0.2	–2.8††	0.9		–0.1	–1.9	1.3	–2.4	not sig
14. Adj. with log *S*	–1.4	0.7	–3.2††	–1.0		–2.4	–2.2	3.2	–3.1†	–††

Differences (Continental Europe–US)

	Food	Chemicals	Oil	Iron and steel	non-ferrous	Engineering (ex. electrical)	Electrical	Autos	Miscellaneous	α-test
1962–7, Full sample										
Biassed										
1. Adj. without log *S*	–0.1	–2.8†	3.0	–0.3	1.7	–4.1††	–4.2**	–0.2	–2.4	–*
2. Adj. with log *S*	1.5	–2.3†	3.1	–0.7	4.5	–3.1	–4.1**	0.0	–2.4	–††
3. Unadj. without log *S*	–7.6†	–0.8	–0.2	2.5	5.5	–5.3††	–4.1*	0.2	–3.2†	–*
4. Unadj. with log *S*	–5.3	–0.1	–1.1	2.2	9.3††	–5.2††	–4.1*	0.8	–3.1	–††
Unbiassed										
5. Adj. without log *S*	–1.0	–4.0*	2.9	–0.7	1.7	–4.6††	–4.6**	–0.7	–3.2	–**
6. Adj. with log *S*	1.6	–3.6††	3.0	–1.5	4.5	–3.0	–4.6**	–0.5	–2.9	–*
1962–67, Reduced sample										
7. Adj. without log *S*	–0.4	0.9	1.5	–0.9		–4.5†	–2.3	–1.2	0.3	not sig.
8. Adj. with log *S*	2.3	0.3	2.0	–3.0†		–5.0††	–2.4	–4.3	–0.1	–†
9. Unadj. without log *S*	–7.6†	3.0	–1.3	3.7†		–4.5†	–3.1	0.5	–0.4	–†
10. Unadj. with log *S*	–5.2	2.0	–3.8	1.2		–5.0††	–3.5	–3.9	–1.0	–††
1957–62										
11. Adj. without log *S*	6.2††	6.3**	0.9	7.3**		3.4†	5.1*	13.7**	13.7**	+**
12. Adj. with log *S*	7.7**	8.1**	1.6	7.3*		5.1*	4.9††	17.8**	3.2	+**
1957–67										
13. Adj. without log *S*	2.9	3.6**	1.2	3.2*		–0.5	1.4	6.4**	7.0*	+**
14. Adj. with log *S*	4.0	4.0††	1.7	1.4		–1.1	0.8	8.1*	3.3	+**

	Differences (Japan–US)								
	Food	Chemicals	Oil	Iron and steel	Engineering (ex. electrical)	Electrical	Autos	Miscellaneous	α-test
1962–67, Full sample									
Biassed									
1. Adj. without log S	8.1††	5.2††	5.3	12.7**	9.3**	–0.9	10.0**	6.7†	+**
2. Adj. with log S	7.8††	3.3	1.9	12.7**	8.9**	–0.9	9.6*	5.7	+**
3. Unadj. without log S	7.7†	4.6	2.1	12.7**	12.7**	–1.3	8.7*	5.8	+**
4. Unadj. with log S	7.4†	2.1	–3.8	12.5**	12.3**	–1.4	7.8*	4.6	+**
Unbiassed									
5. Adj. without log S	7.3†	3.9†	5.7	12.3**	8.8**	–1.3	9.4**	5.9	+**
6. Adj. with log S	6.7†	1.4	1.8	12.1**	8.3**	–1.4	8.9*	3.5	+**
1962–67, Reduced sample									
7. Adj. without log S				12.8**	8.6†				+**
8. Adj. with log S				11.8**	4.8				+**
9. Unadj. without log S				12.8**	8.6†				+**
10. Unadj. with log S				11.6**	4.8				+**
1957–62									
11. Adj. without log S				13.6**	11.1**				+**
12. Adj. with log S				13.6**	12.7*				+**
1957–67									
13. Adj. without log S				13.2**	9.9**				+**
14. Adj. with log S				11.4**	5.7†				+**

Significance. Individual differences. Two-tailed: ** = 1%; * = 5%; †† = 10%; † = 20% levels.

α-test. One tailed. –**, –*, – ††, – † = negative at the 1%, 5%, 10%, 25% levels; +**, +*, +††, +† = positive at the 1%, 5%, 10%, 25% levels.

Differences (UK–US), etc., are the estimated values of the a's in the equations:

without log S $$g_j = e_j + a_{j\,UK} C_{UK} + a_{j\,Eu} C_{Eu} + a_{j\,Ja} C_{Ja} + u_j,$$

with log S $$g_j = e_j + a_{j\,UK} C_{UK} + a_{j\,Eu} C_{Eu} + a_{j\,Ja} C_{Ja} + c_j \log S + d_j \log^2 S + u_j.$$

Table 20 *International differences. (All industries pooled)*

	UK–US	Germany –US	France –US	Benelux –US	Italy–US	EFTA–US	Japan–US	Canada–US	Other–US
1962–7, Full sample									
Biassed									
Adj. without log *S*	–0.8	–3.9**	–1.5	–1.2	–0.6	0.2	6.9**	–0.0	1.4
Adj. with log *S*	–0.8	–2.8*	–1.6	–1.3	0.0	0.2	6.4**	–0.2	0.7
Unadj. with log *S*	–0.7	–4.2**	0.8	–2.3	1.9	–0.7	6.5**	–0.4	2.9
Unadj. with log *S*	–0.6	–3.0*	0.6	–2.5	2.5	–0.9	5.8**	–0.7	1.9
Unbiassed									
Adj. without log *S*	–1.5†	–4.5**	–2.2 †	–1.9	–1.3	–0.5	6.2**	–0.6	–0.9
Adj. with log *S*	–1.6††	–3.1*	–2.3 ††	–2.0	–0.5	–0.7	3.4**	–1.0	–0.1
1962–67, Reduced sample									
Adj. without log *S*	–1.2	–2.3††	–0.4	0.8	1.6	0.1	11.9*	2.8	5.4†
Adj. with log *S*	–1.4	–2.5††	–0.9	0.5	1.3	–0.2	11.6**	2.7	5.1†
Unadj. without log *S*	–0.6	–1.7	1.8	–0.5	6.9*	–1.5	11.0**	3.2	5.4
Unadj. with log *S*	–1.9†	–2.2†	–0.0	–1.7	5.9††	–3.2	10.0**	2.1	3.5
1957–62									
Adj. without log *S*	–0.3	7.6**	5.3**	6.9**	10.2**	5.2**	12.1**	0.7	4.2
Adj. with log *S*	–2.0††	6.4**	2.5†	4.8*	7.9**	2.3	9.3**	–0.6	6.5
1957–67									
Adj. without log *S*	–0.7	2.7**	2.5*	3.8*	5.9**	2.7*	12.0**	1.8	4.7*
Adj. with log *S*	–1.6*	2.0*	1.0	2.7††	4.7*	1.2	10.5**	1.0	2.9

Significance. See Table 13.

Differences (UK–US), etc., are the estimated values of the a_i's in the equations:

without log *S*

$$g = e + \sum_{i=2}^{m} a_i C_i + \sum_{j=1}^{n-1} b_j I_j + u$$

with log *S*

$$g = e + \sum_{i=2}^{m} a_i C_i + \sum_{j=1}^{n} b_j I_j + C \log S + d \log^2 S + u.$$

Table 21 *Annual percentage rates of change in dollar prices.*

	1962–7	1957–62	1957–67
USA	1.2	0.6	0.9
Continental Europe (average)[1]	1.9	1.0	1.4
Germany	1.6	2.6	2.1
France	1.6	–0.8	0.4
Benelux	2.8	0.4	1.6
Italy	2.0	0.0	1.0
Other EFTA	2.2	0.6	1.0
UK	1.4	1.6	1.5
Japan	1.6	0.2	0.8
Canada	2.0	–0.2	0.9

Notes [1] Weighted average. Weights proportional to number of firms in the sample from each country. The reduced and full samples yielded the same average.

Source. OECD. *Main Economic Indicators.*

Part II. Firms and the national economy

6. Firms and the national economy

1. Introduction

International differences in the growth rates of big firms have, as we have seen, been substantial. Moreover, the relative performance of firms of various nationalities changed considerably between 1957–62 and 1962–7. In particular, American firms, having been challenged by the Continental Europeans and the Japanese in the first period, made something of a come-back in the second. An important conclusion of the regressions of Chapter 4 was that only a small part of these differences could be directly explained by international differences in the size of big firms. This does not mean that size did not, in certain industries and at certain times, play its part, nor even that it may not become a crucial factor in the future. It simply means that, during the period we have studied, other factors seem to have been more important. Our aim in this chapter is to examine some of these factors.

The growth of firms is broken down into three components : overseas expansion, the growth of national economies, and domestic concentration. Domestic concentration is the increase in the share of the domestic *output* or *market* enjoyed by a given collection of domestically-owned big firms. The alternative senses in which the concept of domestic concentration is used depend on whether firms' sales are analysed from the demand or supply side, and will be clear in the context of the discussion.

The chapter is divided into two main sections. In the first we examine the extent to which the two kinds of overseas expansion, trade and investment, have affected the firms of various nationalities. In doing so we consider, not only the big firms, but the entire collection of domestically-owned firms. In the second section we discuss how the experience of big firms may differ from that of the average. On the basis of this discussion, we examine the big firms contained in the samples described in previous chapters. The growth of these firms is broken down into two constituents – growth due to the expansion of their domestic economies, and growth due to the combined effects of overseas investments and changing domestic concentration. This shows us how far the growth rates of big firms were determined by the growth rates of their national economies and, in particular, how far the comparative recovery of the Anglo-Saxon firms *vis-à-vis* their continental European rivals was due to the improved performance of the Anglo-Saxon economies.

2. The totality of firms

Overseas expansion

In a world without international trade or investment the growth of firms would be simply and directly related to the growth of national economies. The total output and sales of the firms of any nation would, at all times, be equal to total national output and expenditure. As a result, the total output or sales of firms would *grow* at the same rate as total national production or expenditure. We can express this loosely by saying that the average firm would grow at the same rate as its national economy.[1] An individual firm or group of firms could only grow faster or slower than the national economy if its share of national production or expenditure rose or fell.

When international trade and investment are introduced the picture changes. Sales and output can now be increased by expanding overseas. If it expands fast enough overseas, a firm may be able to combine a higher than average overall rate of growth with a constant or even declining share of the domestic economy.

To give an idea of the part played by overseas expansion in the growth of firms during recent years, we have made the rough estimates given in Table 22.[2]

Table 22 *Gross overseas expansion of manufacturing firms, 1957–65. ($ billions)*

	(1) Δx	(2) ΔO	(3) ΔP	(4) ΔS	(5) $\Delta O/\Delta S$	(6) $\Delta P/\Delta S$
US	4.2	24.0	28.3	183.9	0.13	0.15
UK	3.5	5.4	8.9	27.6	0.20	0.32
France	3.9	0.4	4.3	59.3	0.01	0.07
Germany	8.4	1.4	9.8	62.9	0.02	0.16
Italy	4.0	0.9	4.9	16.6	0.05	0.30
Netherlands	2.0	1.2	3.1	7.2	0.17	0.43
Canada	1.5	0.6	2.1	4.6	0.13	0.46
Japan	5.2	0.6	5.8	29.6	0.02	0.20

For the derivation of this table see Appendix 4

Definitions. Δ = change between 1957 and 1965, X = exports, O = sales of overseas subsidiaries, P = total sales overseas ($X + O$), S = total sales.

Column (1) shows the increase (ΔX) in manufacturing exports between 1957 and 1965 and column (2) the increase (ΔO) in the sales of overseas subsidiaries. Adding these together we get in column (3) an estimate of the increase (ΔP) in overseas sales of manufacturing firms. This estimate suffers from two defects. Firstly, part of the output of overseas subsidiaries is shipped back to the home country. Not all of ΔO, therefore, is sold abroad. Secondly, some exports are produced by foreign-owned subsidiaries operating in the home economy. Thus not all of ΔX represents sales overseas of domestically-owned firms. On both counts ΔP is too high. With the exception of Canada, however, where about half of all manufacturing exports are produced by American subsidiaries, the errors are not likely to be substantial.[3]

To put these estimates in perspective column (4) shows the change ΔS in total sales, at home and abroad, of manufacturing firms. In the last two columns ΔO and ΔP are expressed as proportions of ΔS.

For the UK, the Netherlands, Canada and the US increases in overseas production are relatively important. For their firms, overseas production provided between 13 percent and 20 percent of the total increase in sales. Highest was the UK with 20 percent, a figure which is probably an underestimate.[4] By contrast, the firms of all other countries relied almost entirely on domestic production.

Turning to column (6), we see that the firms of every country except France relied to a substantial extent on foreign markets for their expansion. These markets accounted for between 30 per cent and 50 per cent of the expansion of Canadian, Dutch, Italian and British firms. By contrast, Japanese and German firms, whose export performance has been so striking, relied to a greater extent on home markets where they sold 80 per cent or more of their extra output. Indeed, they do not seem to have been much more directed towards foreign markets than the average American firm, which made up for stagnant exports by investing heavily overseas.

Interpenetration

It is clear from the above discussion that overseas expansion by means of trade and investment has played an important part in the growth of firms. To conclude from this, however, that the process has been one of pure gain for the firms concerned would be a mistake. Overseas expansion is usually a two-way process in which each country both exports and imports goods and capital. For example, manufacturing industrial countries often import about as many manufactures from other industrial countries as they export. Only with the less industrial countries do they have a substantial trade surplus in manufactures. Also, the investing countries are often recipients of foreign direct investment. To show how the entire two-way process of trade and investment has affected the sales and production of the firms of any given country, it is necessary to include losses at home as well as gains abroad. This we do in Table 23 for the period 1957–67.

Suppose that during these years exports of manufactures increased by ΔX and imports by ΔX^*. The overall effect of trade is then a gain in sales overseas of ΔX and a loss at home of ΔX^*. Combining these, we get a net increase through trade of $\Delta X - \Delta X^*$, which we have called Δx.

Next, suppose that domestically-owned subsidiaries increased their sales overseas by ΔO and foreign-owned subsidiaries increased their sales on the home market by ΔO^*. The overall effect of investment on the sales of domestically-owned firms will be a gain overseas of ΔO and a loss at home of ΔO^*. Combining these we get $\Delta O - \Delta O^*$ which we have called Δo.

Thus Δx measures the net expansion via trade and Δo the net expansion via investment of manufacturing firms. Adding these together, we get Δp the net expansion via trade and investment combined.

As might be expected, net expansion is considerably smaller than gross

Table 23 *Net overseas expansion of manufacturing firms, 1957–67 ($ billions)*

	(1) Δx	(2) Δo	(3) Δp	(4) ΔS	(5) $\Delta o/\Delta S$	(6) $\Delta p/\Delta S$
US	–1.8	28.6	26.8	256.2	0.11	0.10
UK	–0.6	2.1	1.5	31.4	0.07	0.05
France	0.4	–1.0	–0.6	72.0	–0.01	–0.01
Germany	6.4	0.8	5.6	64.1	–0.01	0.09
Italy	2.6	–1.7	0.9	23.6	–0.07	0.04
Netherlands	–0.1	0.9	0.8	11.7	0.08	0.07
Canada	0.0	–4.0	–4.0	7.0	–0.57	–0.57
Japan	5.3	5.6	5.6	47.8	0.01	0.12

For the derivation of this table see Appendix 4.

Definitions. For the meaning of X, O, P, and S see Table 22. Let $X^* =$ impor $O^* =$ sales of foreign-owned subsidiaries operating in the home country, $P^* =$ to foreign sales in the home market ($= X^* + O^*$). Net quantities are $x = X - X^*$, $o = O - O^*$, $p = P - P^*$.

expansion. Indeed, in some cases, where inflows are greater than outflows, net expansion is actually negative. Most striking of all is the case of Canada where heavy US investment has caused Δp to be large and negative. Apart from this isolated case, however, the ratios in columns (5) and (6) are fairly small. Viewed statically, taking national production and consumption as given, it seems that the process of interpenetration has had only a limited effect on the growth rate of the average firm. Viewed dynamically, of course, the situation may look quite different. International division of labour and flows of capital and knowledge may have played a crucial role in maintaining post-war capitalist expansion.

The growth of firms

We have just seen that, for the firms of every country except Canada, net expansion through trade and investment was a small proportion of total expansion during 1957–67. As one might expect, this fact is reflected in a relationship between the growth of firms and the growth of national economies.

Let us consider the effect of investment. Suppose we use E to denote the total sales of goods produced by the national economy. A part O^*, of these goods is produced by foreign-owned subsidiaries and the remainder $(E - O^*)$ by domestically-owned firms. The total sales S of domestically-owned firms are, therefore, composed of goods produced at home $(E - O^*)$ and goods produced abroad, O. Thus,

$$S = (E - O^*) + O = E + o, \quad (1)$$

where $\quad o = O - O^*.$

Taking changes over time we get,

$$\Delta S = \Delta E + \Delta o. \quad (2)$$

Equations (1) and (2) can be combined to give, after manipulation, the equation

$$\frac{\Delta S}{S} = \frac{\Delta E}{E}\left(1 + \frac{[(\Delta o/\Delta S) - (o/S)]}{[1 - (\Delta o/\Delta S)]}\right). \qquad (3)$$

This relates the growth rate of firms ($\Delta S/S$) to the growth rate of national production ($\Delta E/E$). It implies that, if the marginal rate of net expansion overseas ($\Delta o/\Delta S$) is greater than the average net expansion (o/S), then $\Delta S/S$ will be greater than $\Delta E/E$, i.e. firms will grow faster on average than their national economy. Conversely, if the marginal rate is less than the average, firms will grow more slowly than their national economy.

It is clear that, unless $1 - (\Delta o/\Delta S)$ is near zero, $\Delta S/S$ and $\Delta E/E$ will be close to each other if $(\Delta o/\Delta S) - (o/S)$ is small. From Table 23 it can be seen that, in the present case, $1 - (\Delta o/\Delta S)$ is never less than 0.89. Thus $\Delta S/S$ and $\Delta E/E$ will be close to each other when $\Delta o/\Delta S - (o/S)$ is small.

Although we do not have estimates of the values of o/S for every country in the table, qualitative arguments are sufficient, for every country except Canada, to show that $(\Delta o/\Delta S) - (o/S)$ is small for the period 1957–67.[5] In the case of Canada both $\Delta o/\Delta S$ and o/S are large and a qualitative argument will not suffice to show that the differences between these two magnitudes is small. Fortunately, published statistics enable us to estimate the value of o/S as being equal to -0.55 in 1957.[6] Since $\Delta o/\Delta S$ is equal to -0.57 we find from Equation (3) that $\Delta S/S = 1.01(\Delta E/E)$. In other words, the total sales at home and abroad of Canadian firms grew at much the same rate as the Canadian economy. Thus for every country on our list $\Delta S/S$ is close to $\Delta E/E$ for the years 1957–67.

This is, of course, a relationship between the production of firms (S) and the production of economies (E). Suppose we denote the total national absorption of manufactures by A. Then we may derive a similar relationship between the sales of firms (S) and national absorbtion (A). To do this we merely repeat the above exercise using p instead of o and A instead of E. Equation (3) then becomes

$$\frac{\Delta S}{S} = \frac{\Delta A}{A}\left(1 + \frac{[(\Delta p/\Delta S) - (p/S)]}{[1 - (\Delta p/\Delta S)]}\right).$$

As before, we can show that $(\Delta p/\Delta S) - (p/S)$ is small and that $\Delta S/S$, therefore, is close to $\Delta A/A$ for the years 1957–67.

Summary

We may sum up this discussion as follows. International trade and investment have weakened the links binding firms to their domestic economies. Overseas sales and, to a lesser extent, overseas production now account for a substantial proportion of the total output of firms. This process of outward expansion has, however, been a two-way affair in which the firms of each advanced industrial country have also lost part of their domestic economies to foreigners. The process has been one of interpenetration in which the net gains or losses have been small in comparison to total expansion. As a result both national production and absorption of manufactures have grown at about the same rate as the total output of nationally owned firms.

3. Big firms

International investment and the big firms

So far we have restricted ourselves to averages and totals covering all the manufacturing firms of a given nationality. This conceals wide variations in the impact of interpenetration on firms. Some have benefited enormously. They have been able to expand their overseas sales and production rapidly at the same time as maintaining or even improving their position in the domestic economy. Others have been less fortunate. Losses in the home economy to foreign firms have outweighed any gains they have been able to make overseas.

Disparities are particularly great in the field of international investment where a few firms, most of them very big, account for the bulk of overseas expansion. Amongst American firms, for example, in 1957 some 143, each with a stake abroad of $25 million or more, accounted for 81 per cent of all American direct investments overseas in manufacturing. Fifteen giants, with an average stake of over $200 million, accounted for more than a third of the total.[7] British investment exhibits a similar concentration. In 1962 some forty-six firms owned 71 per cent of all manufacturing investments overseas.[8] The share of big firms is probably even higher in other countries than in Britain and America. We may assume, therefore, that most of the benefits of overseas investment accrue to a few big firms. By contrast, where investment is a two-way affair in which capital flows inwards as well as outwards, the costs of investment are likely to be borne by a large number of firms. Foreign investment in the home economy intensifies competition and brings with it takeovers as foreign firms try to buy their way into this economy. Many firms, which do not themselves invest overseas, will be affected by this penetration. Foreign firms will capture part of their domestic markets and may even buy out the firms themselves. To the extent this happens and stiffer competition and takeovers affect non-investing firms, the investing firms will have been able to gain the benefits of overseas expansion without paying its costs.

Since investing firms tend to be big and non-investing firms small, we can view interpenetration as a process by which the interests of the small firms of each country are sacrificed to the interests of the big firms of other countries. Big firms, which for political or economic reasons are unable to expand sufficiently at home, expand overseas. As the political price of such expansion they may allow foreign firms to penetrate their own domestic economies. Provided, however, that foreign firms capture the markets and production facilities of smaller domestic firms, this concession will have cost the big firms nothing.

This process could lead to a rise in the level of world-wide concentration at the same time as the level of concentration in each individual economy remains constant or even falls. Consider the example of two countries A and B, between which there is initially no investment. In each country concentration in any industry is measured by the share of national output provided by the three biggest producers. Suppose the three biggest producers of A now invest in B, and those of B invest in A. Moreover, suppose that in each case the original three remain the biggest producers in their home economies and just manage to maintain their share of domestic production. Then, in each individual country the level of concentration, being the share of the three biggest producers, will be exactly the same as it was before investment began. Internationally, however, concentration for the big firms will have increased their share of total output. The big firms of A will have gained at the expense of the small firms of B, and the big firms of B will have gained at the expense of the small firms of A. Thus world-wide concentration will have increased, even though in each individual country it will have remained the same.

To arrive at this result, all we need assume is that the process of international investment leads to a situation where the big firms have gained more overseas than they have lost at home.

In some cases the big firms have managed to increase their domestic shares at the same time as expanding overseas. This may have happened in the United States, for example, during the years 1962–6 and in Britain between 1960 and 1968.[9] In such cases the big firms will have grown considerably faster than their national economies. The small firms, by contrast, will have grown more slowly. They will have lost at home to big domestically-owned firms and, where the inflow of foreign investment has been substantial, they will have also lost to foreign-owned firms.

Thus, although interpenetration has brought fairly small net gains or losses to the totality of firms of any particular country, its benefits for the big firms may have been substantial.

The performance of firms in the samples

A comparison of the growth rates of big firms with the growth rates of their national economies will reveal how far the combined effects of overseas expansion and changes in domestic concentration have been beneficial to big firms. We shall use our two samples for this comparison.

For any particular sample let g_S be the average annual rate of growth of the sales of firms, adjusted to remove the various distortions described earlier.[10] As an index of national output in the relevant sectors let us take value-added in manufacturing and mining, measured in dollars.[11] Let g_E be its annual rate of growth.

In Figs. 5 to 8 g_S is plotted against g_E for various time periods and samples. The solid lines have been fitted by the method of least squares and the broken lines have a slope of 45°. If a point lies above the 45° line the big firms have grown faster than their national economy and the combined effect of domestic concentration and overseas expansion has been beneficial to them. If a point lies below the opposite has been the case.

Both from the diagrams and from the regression results given in Table 24 it is clear that the correlation between g_S and g_E is fairly high. In every case the coefficient of g_E is at least three and a half times its standard error. For the entire ten-year period 1957–67 this coefficient is nearly ten times its standard error and 90 per cent of the variation in g_S is explained by variations in g_E. As we might expect, therefore, growth rates of national economies have exerted a powerful influence on the growth rates of big firms.

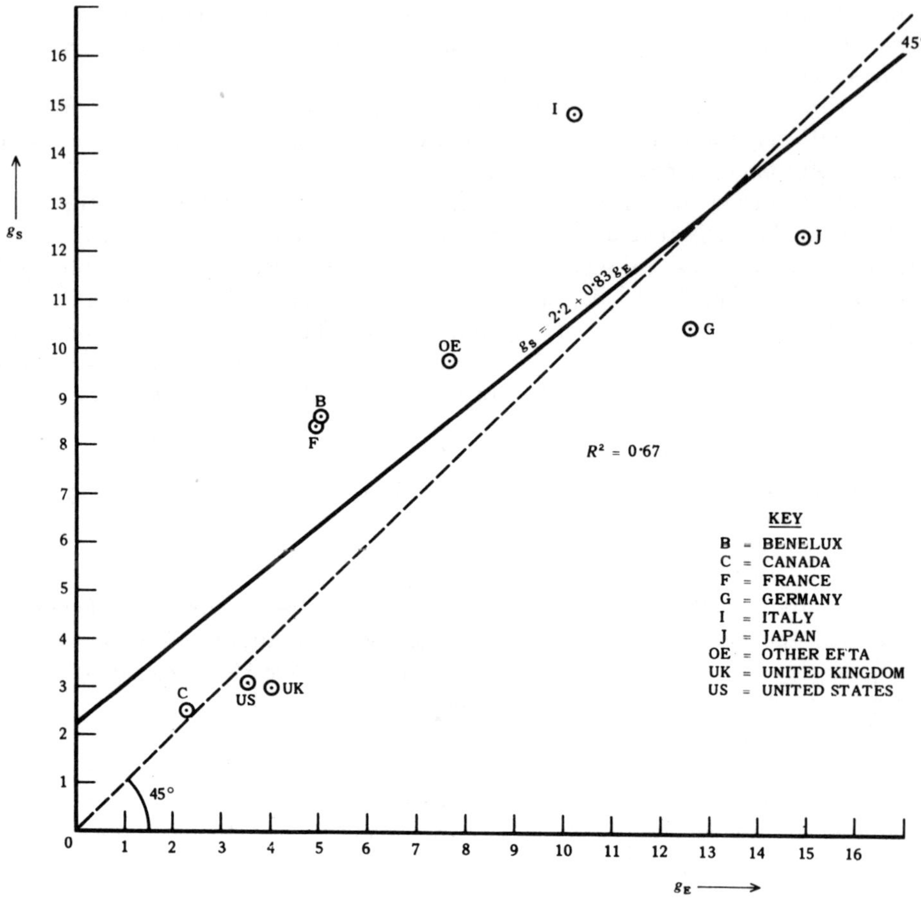

Fig. 5. g_S and g_E : 1957–62

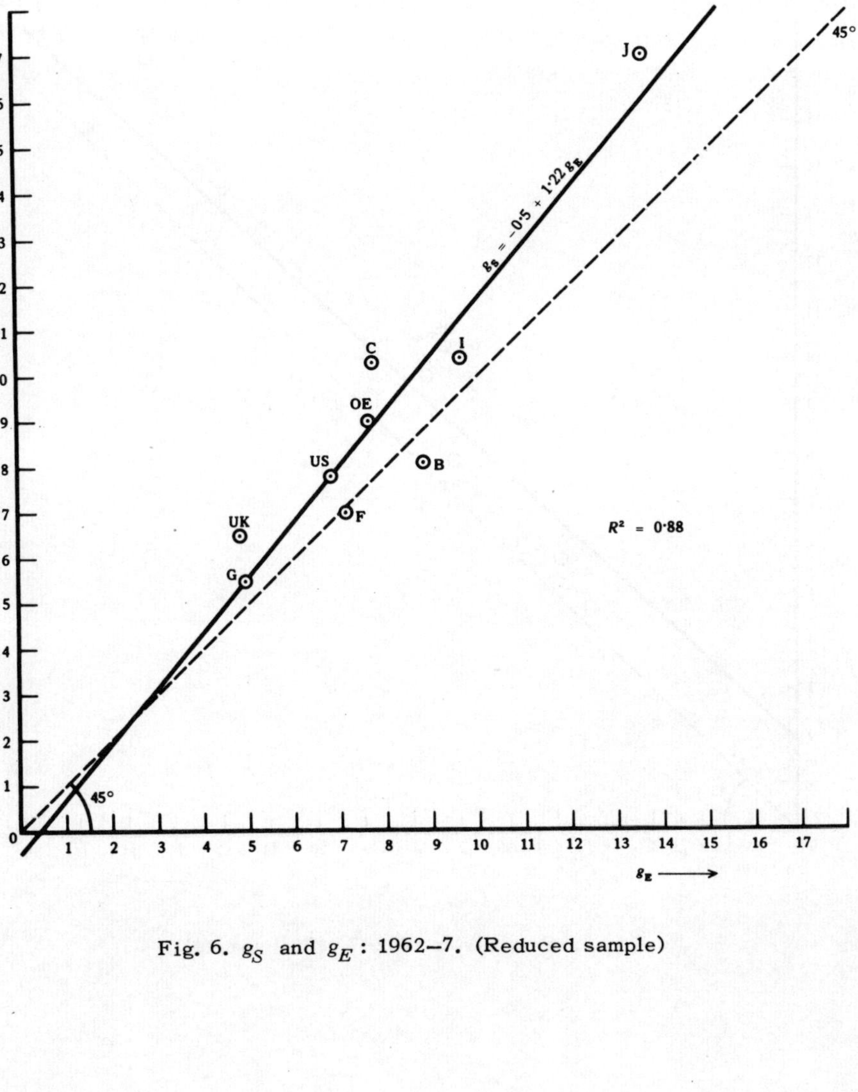

Fig. 6. g_S and g_E : 1962–7. (Reduced sample)

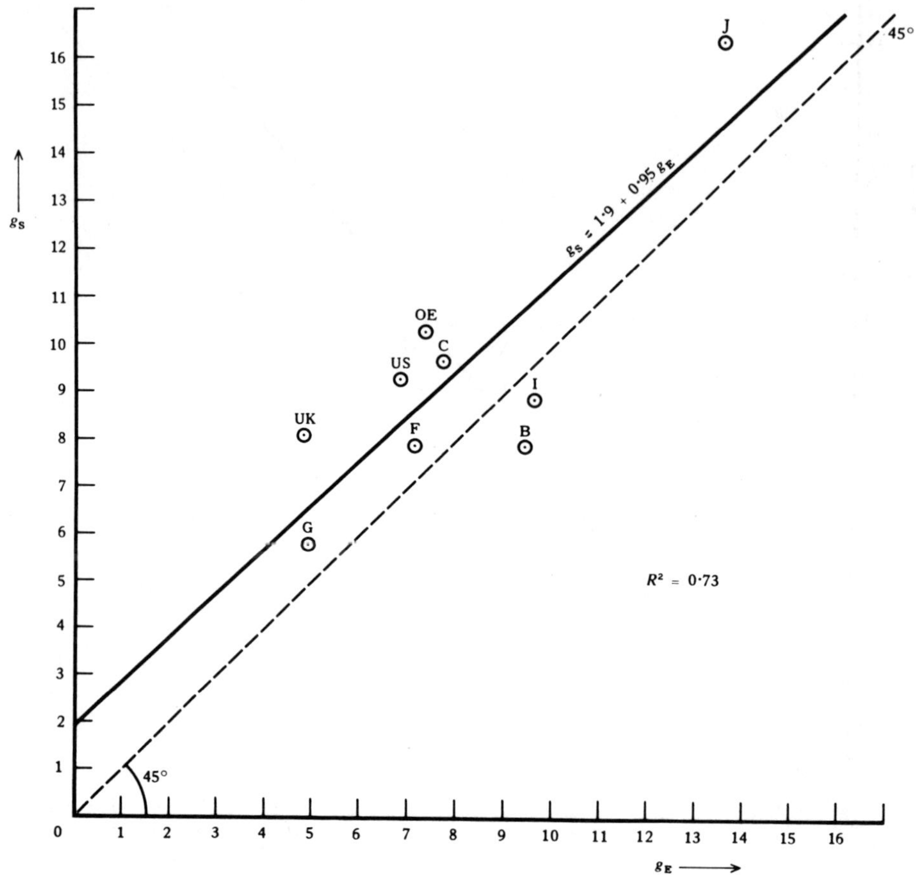

Fig. 7. g_S and g_E : 1962–7. (Full sample)

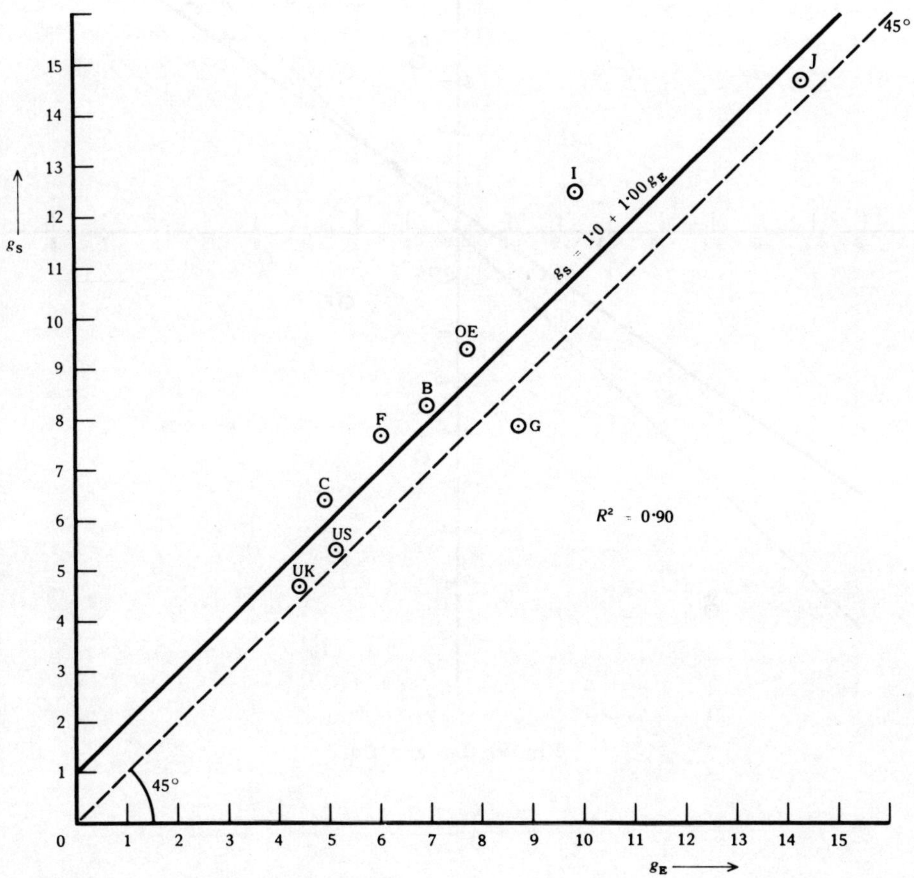

Fig. 8. g_S and g_E : 1957–67

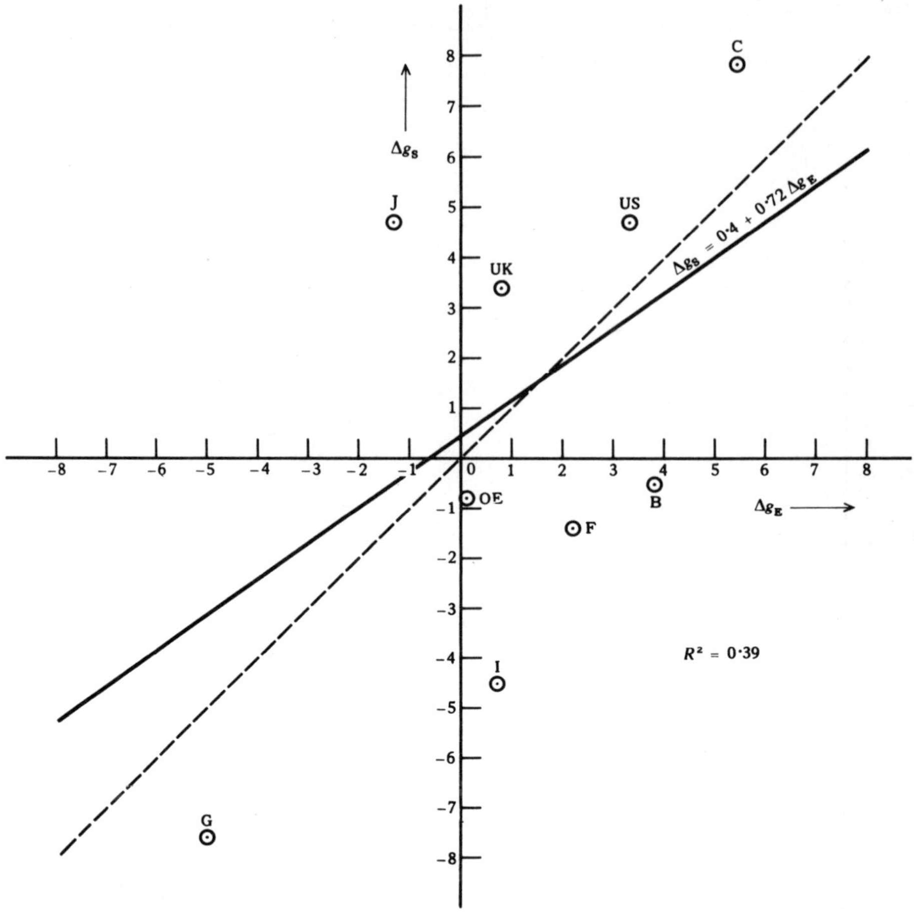

Fig. 9. Δg_S and Δg_E

A striking feature of the diagrams is the tendency for points to lie above the 45° line, particularly in the later period 1962–7, when out of eighteen points in the two samples fourteen lie above the line. Of the remaining four only one lies more than 1 per cent below the line. Over the ten years as a whole the big firms of the reduced sample seem to have grown at an average rate of about 1 per cent a year more than their national economies. Indeed the regression line is exactly parallel to and 1 per cent above the 45° line. Thus there is a distinct tendency for big firms to grow faster than their national economies and we may conclude that the combined effect of overseas investment and domestic concentration has on average been beneficial to big firms.

Table 24 *Regression results*: $g_S = a + bg_E$ [1]

	a	b	R^2
1957–62			
Including Japan	2.2	0.83 (3.77)[2]	0.67
Excluding Japan	1.2	1.03 (3.57)	0.68
1962–7 (reduced sample):			
Including Japan	–0.5	1.22 (7.22)	0.88
Excluding Japan	1.9	0.85 (3.56)	0.68
1962–7 (full sample)			
Including Japan	1.9	0.95 (4.31)	0.73
Excluding Japan	5.5	0.42 (1.45)	0.26
1957–67			
Including Japan	1.0	1.00 (7.80)	0.90
Excluding Japan	0.1	1.14 (5.12)	0.82

[1] g_S = the average rate of growth of adjusted dollar sales of firms in the relevant sample (% p.a.),

g_E = the rate of growth of domestic manufacturing and mining value-added in dollars (% p.a.).

[2] The ratio of b to its standard error is given in brackets, i.e., the t-value.

As one might expect, the correlation is less good for the five-year sub-periods than over the ten years as a whole. Indeed, in the case of the full sample for 1962–7, the correlation seems to be largely due to the existence of one extreme point – Japan. If we exclude Japan, R^2 has a value of 0.26 and the coefficient of g_E is less than one and a half times its standard error. We may conclude that differences in the growth rates of the big firms of Europe and North America during 1962–7 were due far more to different rates of domestic concentration and overseas expansion than to differences in the growth rates of national economies.

This conclusion is confirmed if we look at changes between one five-year period and the next. Changes in g_S do not seem to have been closely related to changes in g_E. This can be seen clearly in Fig. 9 where Δg_S is plotted against Δg_E. The value of R^2 is only 39 per cent, showing that three-fifths of the variation in growth rates between one period and the next must be statistically accounted for by overseas expansion and domestic concentration. Indeed, if the two extreme points – Germany and Canada – are excluded, there appears to be no relationship between Δg_S and Δg_E. It is also clear from Fig. 9 that most of the improved performance of big Anglo-Saxon firms relative to their Continental European rivals cannot be explained by the improved relative growth rates of the Anglo-Saxon economies. The comparative recovery of the Anglo-Saxons must, therefore, have been to a large extent caused by overseas expansion and domestic concentration, although the slowing down of the German economy and the acceleration of the North American economies also played some part.

F

4. Summary

International trade and investment have weakened the links binding firms to their national economies. Overseas sales and, to a lesser extent, overseas production now account for a substantial proportion of the total output of firms. This process of outward expansion has, however, been a two-way affair in which the firms of each advanced industrial country have also lost part of their domestic economy to foreigners. The process has been one of interpretation in which the net gains or losses have been small in comparison to total expansion.

When we look beneath the surface, however, we find that not all firms have had the same experience. The big firms have, as a rule, been able to derive the benefits of overseas investment without paying all of its costs. The influx of foreign capital into their home economies has often harmed not them but smaller firms. A measure of the extent to which the big firms have benefitted from the combined process of overseas investment and domestic concentration is provided by a comparison of their own growth rates with the growth rates of their national economies. Over the ten years 1957–67 the 200 largest firms in the capitalist world grew by an average of about 1.0 per cent a year faster than their national economies. Over short periods of time, moderate differences in national growth rates could be swamped by overseas investment and changes in concentration. Indeed, much of the relative recovery of big American firms seems to have been due more to these factors than to the faster growth of the US economy and the slower growth of the German economy.

7. Large American firms

1. Introduction

In this chapter we examine the contributions of overseas expansion, the growth of the US economy, and changing domestic concentration to the growth of large American firms. This enables us to look at the 'American Challenge' from the point of view of the American firms responsible for this challenge rather than from the more usual European point of view.

2. Growth 1957–66

A recent French publication, *Les investissements directs des Etats-Unis dans le monde,* contains information on the overseas and domestic activities of large American firms in a number of industries.[1] To qualify as large a firm must appear in the *Fortune* top 500. Seven industries, which account for the bulk of US direct investment in manufacturing, are covered in detail: food, paper, chemicals, rubber, metals, electrical and mechanical engineering, and transport equipment. Unfortunately statistics on sales are only given for individual industries for the years up until 1965, although for all seven industries combined they are given for 1966 as well.

The form in which the information is given is not entirely satisfactory as the population changes over time. If new firms enter the top 500 they are included and the slower-growing firms they replace are dropped. Moreover, when two firms in the top 500 merge a new firm is included at the bottom of the list in order to keep the number up to 500. In each case the growth of total sales is biassed upwards. Fortunately, information is given in the form of industry totals and the appearance of a few firms at the lower end of the size scale is not likely to make much difference to these totals.

The total output S^t of large firms at time t is divided into goods produced at home H^t, including exports, and goods produced overseas O^t. Any change in H^t can be decomposed into two components as follows. Suppose total national production changes from E^0 at time 0 to E^1 at time 1. If the share of large firms in national production remained constant their home production would change from H^0 at time 0 to $E^1/E^0.H^0$ at time 1. Let us denote $(E^1/E^0).H^0 - H^0$ by the symbol D_E. Then D_E represents the change in the domestic production of large firms 'caused' by a change in total national production. Let us denote any remaining or 'unexplained' change in their domestic production by D_c. Thus $D_E + D_c = H^1 - H^0$, where D_c is the change due to an increase or decrease in the share of large firms in total national production. Let us also denote the change $O^1 - O^0$ in the overseas production of large firms by D_o. The change in the total production of large firms is made up of the three components D_E, D_C and D_O which satisfy the equations $S^1 - S^0 = D_E + D_C + D_P$.

To facilitate comparisons between industries or between time periods, these components may be expressed as percentages of the absolute change $|S^1 - S^0|$. Thus, using lower-case letters to denote percentages, we shall have $d_E + d_C + d_O = \pm 100$, where the sign is positive when S^1 is greater than S^1 is less than S^0. These definitions and formulae are summarised in Table 25. The intuitive meaning of the *d*'s is clear. The proportion of the growth of large firms accounted for by the growth of the US economy is given by d_E. The proportion accounted for by changes in the share of large firms in this economy is given by d_C, which we can look upon as growth due to domestic concentration. Finally, the proportion of growth accounted for by overseas investment is given by d_O.

The *d*'s decompose growth according to the location of *production*. They do not necessarily tell us very much about the role of particular *markets* in the growth of large firms. To arrive at an accurate decomposition of growth along these lines we should have to take into account imports and exports as well as production. Fortunately, the imports and exports of large American firms are small in comparison with both their home and overseas production. The *d*'s provide, therefore, a fairly reliable picture of the relative importance of home and overseas markets and market shares in the growth of large firms. Thus d_O provides us with a measure of the importance of foreign markets in growth, d_E tells us how important was the expansion of domestic demand, and d_c tells us how important were changes in the domestic market shares of large firms. Only in engineering, where exports accounted for about a third of overseas expansion, will our figures be very inaccurate. In other cases they will be fairly accurate although foreign markets will have been rather more important than our values of d_O suggest, and increases in domestic market shares a little less important than d_c suggests.

Let us now look at the actual values of the various *d*'s, which are given in Table 26A.[2] The values for all industries combined are remarkably similar in the two periods 1957–62 and 1962–5. Rather over half of all growth was accounted for by the expansion of the US economy (d_E), and a further sixth by an increase in the share of large firms in this economy (d_C). The remaining growth, just under a third of the total, was provided by overseas production (d_O). When we look at individual industries the picture is, of course, less clear. The values of *d* vary widely from industry to industry. Over the eight years 1957–65 the contribution of overseas expansion (d_O) varied from 21 per cent in food to 51 per cent in metals. The contribution of domestic concentration (d_c) varied from −46 per cent in rubber to + 26 per cent in paper. Finally, the growth of the US economy (d_E) accounted for between 42 per cent in paper and 116 per cent in rubber.

When we look at variations in the *d*'s between one period and the next the picture is rather confused. The industry values of d_E for 1962–5 are fairly similar to those for 1957–62. When the values of d_E for the later period are regressed against those for the earlier period the value of R^2 is 0.692.[3] It seems that industries which relied most on the growth of the domestic economy

Table 25 *The growth of large US manufacturing firms: formulae*

I *Identity*

$$S^t = H^t + O^t \quad (t = 0, 1.) \tag{1}$$

II *Absolute contributions to growth expansion of the home economy*

$$D = \frac{E^o}{E^o} . H^o - H^o \tag{2}$$

Increased share of the home economy

$$D_c = H^1 - \frac{E^t}{E^o} . H^o \tag{3}$$

Overseas production

$$D_o = O^1 - O^o \tag{4}$$

III *Proportionate contributions to growth (%)*

$$d_E = \frac{D_E . 100}{|S^1 - S^o|}, \quad d_c = \frac{D_c . 100}{|S^1 - S^o|}, \quad d_o = \frac{D_o . 100}{|S^1 - S^o|} \tag{5}$$

From these definitions it follows that,

$$d_E + d_c + d_o = \pm 100 \tag{6}$$

List of symbols:

S^t = Total production of large US firms.

H^t = Home production of large US firms.

O^t = Overseas production of large US firms.

E^t = Total production of the home economy, including the output of foreign-owned subsidiaries.

D_E = Increase in the home production of large US firms, assuming their share of total home production remains constant.

D_c = Increase in the home production of large US firms due to a change in their share of total home production (i.e. to concentration).

D_o = Increase in overseas production of large US firms.

d_E, d_c, d_o, = D_E, D_c, D_o expressed as percentages of the absolute change in production $|S^1 - S^o|$.

in one period did so in the next, and *vice versa*. No such continuity is visible, however, when we look at concentration. The values of d_C for the second period are almost uncorrelated with those for the first.[4] Moreover, three of the seven values are of different signs in the two periods. Thus, although concentration was on average a major source of growth, its importance for individual industries varied considerable from one period to the next. Paper, for example, had the highest value of d_C in 1957–62, yet in 1962–5 was bottom of the list with a negative value. Metals, on the other hand, had the most negative value in 1957–62, yet had the third highest positive value in 1962–5.

The values of d_O for 1962–5 are also uncorrelated with the values for 1957–62.[5] There is no clear pattern by which some of the seven industries re ly regularly on overseas expansion for an above-average proportion of their growth and others for a below-average proportion. More important than the correlation, however, is the important of overseas investment for every single industry in each time period. For no industry, at no time, does the value of d_O fall below 17 per cent and, over the nine years 1957–65 as a whole, d_O does not fall below 21 per cent.[6]

Thus, in all seven industries and in both time periods, the growth of the US economy and overseas expansion were important sources of growth for large firms. Concentration, on the other hand, although, on average, important in each period, was a more unstable and irregular source of growth.

Towards the end of the period in 1965 and even more in 1966 the share of big firms in domestic production began to expand rapidly. As a result overseas production, although still growing very fast became relatively less important, accounting for only 22 per cent of the growth of big firms in the seven industries combined during 1962–6. Domestic concentration accounted for 29 per cent of total growth.

It is instructive to see how fast overseas production had to grow to account for even a third or less of total expansion. In Table 26B we see that total overseas production rose by an average rate of 14 per cent a year during 1962–6. Over the nine-year period 1957–66 it grew by 11.1 per cent a year. In some industries the figures were particularly high being12.4 per cent a year during 1957–65 for transport equipment and 13.9 per cent for chemicals. In these industries, overseas production accounted for about one and a half times as much growth as domestic concentration.

The reason for this state of affairs was, of course, the low proportion of total output produced overseas. From Table 26C we can see that, even as late as 1965, there was no industry in which overseas production accounted for as much as a third of the total output of the big firms. The average proportion was under a fifth. In such a situation a comparatively small proportionate increase in domestic production is equivalent to a large proportionate increase in overseas production. Between 1957 and 1966, for example, overseas production grew by nearly 4 per cent a year faster than the domestic production of large firms, yet the difference between the growth (g_S) of the total production of these firms and the growth (g_H) of their domestic production was 0.6 per cent a year. In no single industry was the difference more than 1.2 per cent a year. Thus, over the period as a whole, the growth of large American firms was mainly determined by events in the domestic economy.

However, it should be recognised that fundamental changes in economic structure result from the persistance of small differentials compounded over long periods of time. Thus differentials in growth rates in overseas markets of the kind observed for the period 1957–66 will have a cumulative effect; moreover, as the relative importance of overseas investment slowly increases a given differential in growth will have greater impact.

During the period of most rapid overseas expansion, 1962–6, increases in domestic concentration outweighed overseas expansion as a source of growth. It will be of interest to ask what the effects on the relative position of American and European firms would be of a decline in the impetus to growth of increasing domestic concentration in the US. Let us speculate on this possibility by looking at an example in which there is no increase in domestic concentration in the US, but in which energies and resources otherwise devoted to increasing concentration are utilised to achieve equal expansion overseas.

At what rate would the Americans need to expand faster overseas to compensate for their stagnant domestic share? To maintain their overall rate of growth during 1962–6, overseas production would have grown at 28.6 per cent p.a. instead of its actual rate of 14.0 per cent p.a.

Alternatively, without increases in domestic concentration, but with the actual overseas expansion at 14.0 per cent p.a. American firms would have grown during 1962–6 at 8.5 per cent p.a. instead of their actual achievement of 12.0 per cent p.a. Thus without the element of increasing domestic concentration there would have been no 'American Challenge' – large American firms would have grown at the same rate as their European rivals, or perhaps, more slowly.

The degree of dependence on the home economy in 1966 is indicated by the fact that a decline in the growth rate of US economy of 1 per cent, 2 per cent or 3 per cent p.a. would require an increase in the rate of growth of overseas production of 4 per cent, 8 per cent and 12 per cent p.a. respectively to compensate for it.

It is clear from these examples that large American firms are still closely dependent on events in the domestic economy. Domestic concentration over the years 1957–66 was just as important a source of growth as overseas expansion. The growth of the US economy was as important as these two two combined. Any fall in the relative rate of growth of the US economy will force large American firms either to increase their share of domestic economy rapidly, or else expand overseas at a truly colossal rate if they are not to fall behind their rivals overseas.

3. Evidence from the full and reduced samples

An interesting divergence between the experience of the 'giants' of the top 100 and the remaining large firms emerges when we consider the growth rates of large American firms in the reduced and full samples. The top 100 American firms of the reduced sample grew by about 1 per cent a year faster than the US economy during 1962–7. As these firms were expanding rapidly overseas during this period, this 1 per cent must have been largely the result of overseas expansion, whilst their share in domestic economy could not have increased much. The remaining firms of the full sample in the range 100–300, on the other hand, grew at nearly 4 per cent a year faster than the US economy. Since overseas expansion could not have accounted for more than a fraction of this gap, it is almost certain that their domestic share expanded fairly rapidly.

If this description is correct we have the following hypothesis. The 'giants' were unable to increase their share of the domestic economy and compensated partially for their stagnant share by expanding overseas. The remaining large firms, on the other hand, were able to raise their domestic shares rapidly and did not rely on overseas expansion to anything like the same extent.

Although these hypotheses will not be discussed in detail two possible explanations are worth mentioning. The stagnant domestic share of the 'giants' may have been due either to their inability to compete at home, or else to the constraints resulting from anti-trust laws. These correspond, respectively to *economic* and *political* constraints. If economic constraints were responsible then the ability of the remaining large firms to increase their domestic share reflects their superior competitive power *vis-à-vis* the 'giants'. If political constraints were responsible, however, this need not have been the case. The 'giants' might have been economically powerful enough to grow faster at home but were prevented from doing so by the political power of smaller firms and other anti-trust forces.

Whatever the causes, however, political or economic, the 'giants' do not seem to be able to increase their domestic share significantly, and overseas expansion is the only way in which they can grow faster than the US economy. So far, the other large firms have been able to grow faster than the US economy by increasing their domestic share. As time goes by, however, this will become increasingly difficult and they, like the 'giants' will be compelled either to grow at the more or less same rate as their domestic economy or else expand very rapidly overseas.

4. Summary

An analysis of the growth of American manufacturing firms in the top 500 revealed that, between 1957 and 1966, roughly a quarter was provided by overseas expansion and three-quarters by domestic growth. Of domestic growth two-thirds was due to the growth of the American economy and the remaining third was due to the increased share of big firms in that economy. Thus concentration was on average about as important for big US firms as overseas expansion. There is some evidence to suggest that the relative importance of these two factors was not the same for the 'giants' as for the remaining big firms. The 'giants' probably relied more on overseas expansion than on domestic concentration, whereas the other big firms probably relied more on concentration. Whatever the truth in these rather speculative conclusions, one thing is certain. If the big American firms are prevented, by political or economic obstacles, from increasing their domestic share rapidly, they will become liable to grow more slowly than their foreign rivals in the event of any slowing down of the US economy. If the economies of the other advanced capitalist countries continue to grow substantially faster than the US economy, big American firms will have to expand overseas at a high rate if they are not to be overtaken by foreign rivals.

Table 26 *The growth of large US firms*[1 2]

A. Contributions to growth (% of total)[3]

	1957–62			1962–5			1957–65		
	Expansion of US economy (d_E)	Concentration (d_c)	Overseas production (d_o)	Expansion of US economy (d_E)	Concentration (d_c)	Overseas production (d_o)	Expansion of US economy (d_E)	Concentration (d_c)	Overseas production (d_o)
By industry									
Food	82	–7	25	82	1	17	83	–4	21
Paper	34	47	19	64	–10	46	42	26	32
Chemicals	57	11	32	47	23	30	51	19	30
Rubber	101	–36	35	118	–44	26	116	–46	30
Metals	+25*	–176*	+51*	55	16	29	86	–37	51
Engineering (elec and mech)	61	18	21	63	12	25	60	17	23
Transport equipment	37	28	35	52	20	28	45	25	30
All seven industries †	53	15	32	55	17	28	54	17	29

* Total sales fell between 1957 and 1962. Thus $S^1 - S^0 < 0$

† For 1962–6 the corresponding figures were: 49, 29, 22.
For 1957–66 they were: 49, 26, 25.

1 Size is measured by the gross value of output which is assumed to be equal to sales measured in current US dollars.

2 Large firms are those included in the *Fortune* 500.

3 For the meaning of the various symbols see the list under Table 25.

Table 26 (continued) *B. Growth rates (% p.a.). Output of large US firms: growth rates*[1]

	1957–62				*1962–5*				*1957–65*			
	US Economy (g_E)	Home (g_H)	Overseas (g_O)	Total (g_S)	US economy (g_E)	Home (g_H)	Overseas (g_O)	Total (g_S)	US economy (g_E)	Home (g_H)	Overseas (g_O)	Total (g_S)
By industry												
Food	3.7	3.4	6.2	3.8	6.4	6.4	6.7	6.5	4.7	4.5	6.4	4.8
Paper	3.8	8.2	6.0	7.7	7.1	6.1	15.5	8.4	5.0	7.4	9.5	8.0
Chemicals	4.8	5.6	12.8	6.9	7.0	10.1	15.9	11.3	5.7	7.3	13.9	8.5
Rubber	5.2	3.5	6.5	4.2	11.0	7.2	8.1	7.4	7.3	4.9	7.1	5.4
Metals	0.3	–2.0	5.7	–1.2	5.5	7.1	17.8	8.6	2.2	1.3	10.1	2.4
Engineering (elec. and Mech)	4.5	5.7	8.8	6.2	7.8	9.2	15.1	10.2	5.7	7.0	11.2	7.7
Transport equipment	2.2	3.6	9.6	4.6	8.4	11.3	17.2	12.5	4.4	6.4	12.4	7.5
All seven industries		*1957–62*				*1962–66*				*1957–66*		
	3.0	3.8	8.9	4.6	7.8	11.6	14.0	12.0	5.1	7.2	11.1	7.8

[1] Growth rates are denoted by g with a subscript. For the meaning of E, H, O, S see the list of symbols under table 25.

Table 26 (continued) *C. Proportion of total sales accounted for by overseas subsidiaries (%)*[1]

By industry	*1957*	*1962*	*1965*
Food	14.6	16.4	16.5
Paper	25.2	23.3	28.3
Chemicals	15.4	20.2	22.8
Rubber	21.0	23.5	23.6
Metals	9.2	12.8	16.4
Engineering (elec. and mech.)	14.3	16.2	18.5
Transport equipment	15.3	19.3	21.8
	1957	*1962*	*1966*
All seven industries	15.1	18.3	19.6

Source: *Travaux et Recherches*, La Documentation Francaise, Paris 1969.

[1] Equals O^t/S^t.

Conclusions

Part I

The first part of this study consisted of an econometric analysis of the growth of the 500 largest industrial firms in the capitalist world during the years 1957–67. The broad conclusionsof the analysis were as follows.

Size and growth

1. Amongst smaller US firms, with sales in the range $ 150 million to $ 500 million, the percentage rate of growth seems to have been a decreasing function of size in 1962–7. Amongst non-US firms this may also have been the case, but this is uncertain as the observed negative relationship might have been caused by biasses. It was not possible to test the relationship amongst smaller firms during 1957–62 or 1957–67 as a whole because only the reduced sample of firms was available.

2. Amongst medium and large firms growth may have been a decreasing function of size in both 1957–62 and 1962–7. The evidence, however, for this conclusion is weak.

3. At no time, and in no area, are there signs of the percentage growth rate being an increasing function of size.

Thus for firms with sales above $ 500 million a year, growth and size seem to be unrelated to each other.

Nationality and growth

1. Japanese firms were clear leaders in each time-period and in almost every industry.

2. In 1957–62 the Continental European firms were next, being well ahead of the Americans. In 1962–7 the American firms recovered and grew as fast in most industries as the Continentals, and considerably faster in electricals and engineering. Over the ten years 1957–67 as a whole, however, the Americans grew more slowly than the Continentals in seven out of eight industries. Only in electricals, engineering and oil did they perform comparatively well.

3. The Anglo-Saxon firms – the British, Canadians and Americans – were closely bunched throughout. In 1957–62 they all grew substantially more slowly than the Continentals, and in 1962–7 they all recovered. The British in 1962–7 grew somewhat more slowly than the Americans, although over the ten years 1957–67, as a whole, there was not much to choose between them.

4. There did seem to be an 'American Challenge' to the European firms in electricals and, to a lesser extent, in engineering in 1962–7. This should, however, be put into perspective by looking at the performance during 1957–62 and in other industries during 1962–7. In chemicals, oil, and autos, which may be considered 'modern' industries, there was no clear American lead in 1962–7, and in some cases there seemed to be a European lead. Moreover, during the years 1957–67, as a whole, the American firms grew more slowly than the continentals in seven out of eight industries, and at about the same rate as the British. Finally, when we look only at very large firms in the electrical industry the American superiority in growth is greatly reduced and is not statistically significant.

5. The smaller American firms with sizes in the range of $ 150 million to $ 500 million grew faster than the larger. Amongst the large firms the Americans did not have a clear lead even in 1962–7 over either the British or the Continentals.

Thus during 1962–7 the American firms grew faster than the European in electricals, and to a lesser extent in engineering. There are signs, therefore, of an 'American Challenge' in these industries. Overall, however, the American and European firms grew at much the same rate in 1962–7, and over the period 1957–67 the Continentals grew much faster. The larger size of American firms does not seem to have been an advantage. On the contrary, it was the smaller American firms with sales in the range $ 150 million to $ 500 million which grew fastest.

Part II

The second part of the study attempted to put the results of the econometric analysis into perspective. International differences in the growth rates of large firms were related to the growth rates of their domestic economies, their rates of overseas expansion, and to the behaviour of their shares in their domestic economies. This relationship was examined in detail for American firms. The broad conclusions of this part were as follows.[1]

Firms and the national economy

International trade and investment have weakened the links binding firms to their national economies. Overseas sales and, to a lesser extent, overseas production now account for a substantial proportion of the total output of firms. This process of outward expansion has, however, been a two-way affair in which the firms of each advanced industrial country have also lost part of their domestic economy to foreigners. The process has been one of interpenetration in which the net gains or losses have been small in comparison with total expansion.

Not all firms have had the same experience. The big firms have, as a rule, been able to derive the benefits of overseas expansion without paying all of its costs. The influx of foreign capital into their home economies has often harmed not them, but smaller firms. A measure of the extent to which the big firms have benefitted from the combined process of overseas investment and domestic concentration is provided by a comparison of their own growth rates with the growth rates of their national economies. Over ten years from 1957–67 the top 200 largest firms of the capitalist world grew by an average of about 1.0 per cent a year faster than their national economies. Over short periods of time moderate differences in national growth rates could be swamped by overseas investment and changes in concentration. Indeed, the relative recovery of big American firms seems to have been due more to these factors than to the faster growth of the US economy and the slower growth of the German economy.

Large American firms

An analysis of the growth of American manufacturing firms in the top 500 revealed that, between 1957 and 1966, roughly a quarter was provided by overseas expansion and three-quarters by domestic growth. Of domestic growth two-thirds was due to the growth of the American economy and the remaining third to the increased share of big firms in that economy. Thus concentration was, on average, about as important for big US firms as overseas expansion. There is some evidence that the relative importance of these two factors was not the same for the giants as for the remaining big firms. The giants probably relied more on overseas expansion than on domestic concentration, whereas the other big firms probably relied more on concentration. One thing is certain; if the big American firms are prevented, by political or economic obstacles, from increasing their domestic share rapidly, they will become liable to grow more slowly than their foreign rivals in the event of any slowing down of the US economy. If the economics of the other advanced capitalist countries continue to grow substantially faster than the US economy, big American firms will have to expand overseas at a high rate if they are not to be overtaken by their rivals.

Appendix 1
Bias

Bias

The results of Chapters 4 and 5 are based upon data given in the *Fortune* lists. The incomplete nature of these data may lead to biasses which can be considered under two headings: *deletions* and *mergers*.

Deletions

The *Fortune* lists give information on the sales of the top 500 US and the top 200 non-US firms for the years 1962–7. The full sample used for many of the regressions consists roughly of the top 300 US and the top 200 non-US firms. Thus all available non-American firms are included in the full sample but only three-fifths of available American firms. This implies that small, slow-growing US firms at the bottom end of the sample are treated differently from their non-US equivalents. A slow-growing American firm which dropped out of the top 300 by 1967 will have remained on the *Fortune* list. We shall have information on the sales of this firm for the entire five-year period 1962–7 and it will, therefore, be included in the full sample. A slow-growing non-American firm, on the other hand, which dropped out of the top 200 will no longer be present on the *Fortune* list. Thus the full sample excludes a number of small, slowly-growing non-US firms but includes their US equivalents.

Therefore any comparison based upon the full sample excludes some slow-growing non-US firms and will give the impression that non-US firms are growing faster than they really are. These firms are also *small* and therefore *small* firms will appear to be growing faster than they really are. The situation is summarised in the first line of Table 27.

There are several ways in which we can remove one or other of these biasses. The non-US bias springs from the fact that we excluded some slow-growing non-American firms but included their American equivalents. If we exclude the slow-growing American firms as well then, although both American and non-American growth rates will be biassed upwards, there will no longer be any bias in *relative* growth rates. This method has, however, a serious disadvantage. By dropping some extra small slow-growing firms we shall increase the upward bias in the growth rates of small firms. The situation is summarised in the second line (Sample B) of Table 27.

To remove the small-firm bias we can construct a new sample as follows. Instead of including all non-US firms for which we have information, suppose we restrict the sample to those non-US firms which were amongst the Y largest in 1962, where Y is a small enough number to ensure that no firm grows so slowly that it fails to appear in the top 200 in 1967. To preserve some kind

Table 27 *Samples and biasses caused by deletions*

Sample	Small slowly-growing firms US	Small slowly-growing firms non-US	Biasses caused by deletions non-US	Biasses caused by deletions Small	Sample size US	Sample size non-US
A (full sample)	included	excluded	+	+	280	158
B	excluded	excluded	0	++	263	158
C (reduced sample)	included	included	0	0	97	77
D	included	included	0	0	197	125

of balance and to prevent the sample being dominated by the American firms we can restrict ourselves to a smaller number of Americans, say the X largest in 1962.

How do we choose X and Y? The maximum we can make Y without including firms which are not in the top 200 in 1967 is 137. Given this value of Y we can choose any value of X. Suppose we include only American firms whose sales in 1962 were greater than or equal to those of the 137th non-American. Then X will be equal to 209. After dropping firms because of mergers or some other reason we are left with 197 US and 125 non-US firms. This we have called sample D. To use sample D, however, would lead to an excessive proliferation of samples and regressions. In addition to the three samples discussed so far we should also have the reduced sample, which is used for 1957–62 and 1957–67. Fortunately, the reduced sample itself leads to unbiassed estimates. All of its non-US firms are sufficiently large to appear in the *Fortune* list in 1967, no matter how slowly they grew. It appears in Table 27 as Sample C.

Mergers

Biasses may also be caused by our treatment of mergers. *Fortune* mentions mergers only when both firms concerned appeared on the list in the previous year. To see how this may lead to biasses consider the following example. Suppose a firm A merges with a firm B which is half its size. If A is large and near the top of the list then B will also be fairly large and will also be in the *Fortune* list. Adjustments will therefore remove the effects of this merger. If, on the other hand, A is small and near to the bottom of the *Fortune* list, then B will be so small that it will not be on the list. Adjustment will not remove the effect of this merger. Adjustment will, in these circumstances, lead to an upward bias in the *relative* growth rates of small firms. The smaller our sample is compared to the original list, the less important will such biasses be. The reduced sample, which is drawn from the top 100 US and the top 100 non-US firms, should limit bias from this source.

If, on the other hand, we rely on the full sample, then, amongst the non-American firms, there may be an upward bias in the growth rates of small firms. Mergers between firms at the bottom of the list and firms a little smaller than these will not be mentioned by *Fortune*. Their effects, therefore, will not be removed by adjustment. This problem also arises amongst the American firms of the full sample. In many cases, however, mergers involve other firms in the top 500 and, as a result, the bias will be much less than amongst the non-American firms. Thus, when the full sample is used, adjustment is likely to produce an upward bias in the relative growth rates of small firms, which is larger for the non-Americans than the Americans. We observed something similar when considering biasses caused by the exclusion of small, slow-growing non-American firms. As before, the result will be a positive small-firm bias amongst the non-Americans and a positive bias in the growth rates of the non-American firms as a whole. There will also be a positive small firm bias amongst the Americans of the full sample, which we assume is small enough to be ignored.

The combined biasses

When we combine both kinds of bias the result is given by Table 28.

Table 28 *The combined biasses*

	Small firms bias			
	US	non-US	world	non-US bias
Full sample	0	++	+	+
Sample B	++	++	++	0
Reduced sample	0	0	0	0

Although it leads to unbiassed results, the reduced sample has two disadvantages. It contains fewer firms, and some of the estimates derived from it may therefore be unreliable because of their high variance. Moreover, the reduced sample excludes American firms in the range 100–300 and non-American firms in the range of 100–200. This is the area in which size effects seem to be most important. Thus the reduced sample eliminates bias, but only at the cost of increasing the variance of estimates and of restricting coverage.

Are the biasses important?

As the biasses arise from lack of information it is not possible to evaluate them directly. We can, however, get a rough idea of their importance by looking at data for the United States.

To estimate the magnitude of merger bias all we need do is ignore any information contained in *Fortune* about mergers with firms in the bottom 200 and proceed with adjustments as before. Using this newly adjusted data we repeat our American regressions to arrive at the biassed results given in Table 29 under the heading *Effects of Mergers*. By comparing these biassed results with their unbiassed equivalents we estimate the bias.

If *Fortune* had given no information on the bottom 200 American firms then we should have been forced to drop seventeen American firms which had grown so slowly that they had ended up in the bottom 200 in 1967. To estimate the magnitude of this bias all we need do is drop the seventeen firms from the full sample of American firms and repeat the American

G

regressions. The biassed redults, using data adjusted in the usual way, are given in Table 29 under the heading *Effects of Deletions.* By comparing these with their unbiassed equivalents we can estimate the bias.

Finally, to estimate the combined bias all we need do is combine the above methods. We ignore information about mergers with firms in the bottom 200 and drop any firms which appeared in the bottom 200 in 1967. The biassed results are given in Table 29, under the heading *Combined Effects.* Once again we can estimate the bias by comparing these with their unbiassed equivalents.

To display these biasses in a way which makes them comparable with the results given in Chapter 4 we calculate the estimated values taken by $Z = dg/d(\log S)$ for maximum and minimum values of S. These are called $\hat{Z}_{max}$ and $\hat{Z}_{min}$ respectively. A full discussion of these terms is given in Chapter 2.

Two features stand out clearly in Table 29. Deletions frequently lead to a substantial bias, whereas the exclusion of mergers with firms in the bottom 200 does not. In every industry deletions lead to a negative bias in $\hat{Z}_{min}$ and a positive bias in $\hat{Z}_{max}$. When all industries are combined $\hat{Z}_{min}$ has an unbiassed value of –3.4 per cent and a biassed value of –4.9 per cent, a change of –1.5 per cent. The corresponding change in $\hat{Z}_{max}$ is 2.3 per cent. By contrast, the effect of mergers is much less clear cut. Sometimes $\hat{Z}_{min}$ increases and $\hat{Z}_{max}$ decreases, and sometimes the opposite happens. Moreover, the changes are never very large. Thus it makes comparatively little difference whether we exclude mergers with firms in the bottom 200.

Where a number of firms in one industry are affected the combined bias may be quite striking. In food, for example, when both kinds of bias are combined the value of $\hat{Z}_{min}$ changes from +1.0 per cent to –6.6 per cent and $\hat{Z}_{max}$ from –3.6 per cent to +1.5 per cent. Overall, $\hat{Z}_{min}$ experiences a bias of –2.2 per cent and $\hat{Z}_{max}$ a bias of +2.3 per cent. It is interesting to see what biasses of this magnitude would have meant for European firms. For them the values of $\hat{Z}_{min}$ and $\hat{Z}_{max}$ obtained, when all industries were pooled, were –3.5 per cent and +0.4 per cent respectively. Assume these estimates have biasses equal to the American combined biassed of –2.3 per cent and +2.3 per cent respectively. The corresponding unbiassed values will then be –1.3 per cent for $\hat{Z}_{min}$ and –1.9 per cent for $\hat{Z}_{max}$. With these values $Z = dg/d(\log S)$ will be negative over the entire range of observed sizes, and g will be a uniformly decreasing function.

Summary

The choice of sample and treatment of mergers caused some biasses. These biasses were probably serious in the case of the full sample of European firms, but in other cases they were not serious. It is possible that most of the observed negative relationships between growth and size amongst European firms were spurious due to bias. The true relationship was, perhaps, one in which growth diminished slowly and uniformly with size. This conclusi is not, however, certain. The only thing that does appear to be fairly certain is that amongst the European firms growth was nowhere a significantly increasing function of size.

Table 29 *Bias. (US firms, 1962–7)*

	Food	Chemical	Oil	Iron and steel	non-ferrous	Engineering (ex. electrical)	Electrical	Autos	Miscellaneous	All
No. of firms	44	39	21	13	12	33	32	17	69	280
Effect of deletions										
No. of deletions	5	3		1		1			7	17
$\hat{Z}_{min}$ (% p.a.): Unbiassed	1.0	–7.8		–0.2		–1.2			0.7	–3.4
Biassed	–2.4	–9.7		–3.0		–3.3			–1.6	–4.9
$\hat{Z}_{max}$ (% p.a.): Unbiassed	–3.6	2.6		–1.7		–2.6			–2.3	1.8
Biassed	–1.7	3.1		–0.1		–1.1			–1.4	3.5
Effect of mergers										
No. of mergers	3	3	3			1	3	1	2	16
$\hat{Z}_{min}$ (% p.a.): Unbiassed	1.0	–7.8	–9.4			–1.2	–3.8	–3.3	0.7	–3.4
Biassed	–1.2	–7.6	–9.0			–1.2	–2.6	–3.4	–2.3	–3.8
$\hat{Z}_{max}$ (% p.a.): Unbiassed	–3.6	2.6	5.9			–2.6	0.7	1.9	–2.3	1.8
Biassed	–2.0	1.6	5.8			–3.0	–0.8	1.5	–0.2	2.2
Combined effect										
No. of mergers and deletions	8	6	3	1		2	3	1	9	33
$\hat{Z}_{min}$ (% p.a.): Unbiassed	1.0	–7.8	–9.4	–0.2		–1.2	–3.8	–3.3	0.7	–3.4
Biassed	–6.6	–9.7	–9.0	–3.0		–3.3	–2.6	–3.4	–6.0	–5.6
$\hat{Z}_{max}$ (% p.a.): Unbiassed	–3.6	2.6	5.9	–1.7		–2.6	0.7	1.9	–2.3	1.8
Biassed	1.5	2.2	5.8	–0.1		–1.4	–0.8	1.5	1.6	4.1

Appendix 2
The α - test

The α-test

Suppose we conduct n independent experiments whose outcomes are described by the real numbers $t_1, \ldots t_n$. Suppose also that, if the null hypothesis H_o is as assumed to be correct, these outcomes have known, continuous, but not necessarily identical, cumulative probability distributions given by:

$$F_i(k_i) = P(t_i \leqslant k_i) \quad (i = 1, \ldots n).$$

For any set of outcomes $k_1, \ldots, k_n$ let us define a new set of variables p_i given by:

$$p_i(k_i) = F_i(k_i) \quad (i = 1, \ldots n).$$

In effect we are replacing each k_i by the conditional probability that, if the null hypothesis is correct, the ith experiment will yield an outcome t_i no greater than the outcome k_i actually observed.

It is easy to show that each of the p_i's will have the uniform distribution whose density function f is given by:

$$\begin{aligned} f(p_i) &= 1 \text{ for } o < p_i < 1, (i = 1, \ldots n) \\ &= o \text{ otherwise.} \end{aligned}$$

Moreover, it is obvious that the p_i's are independent of each other.

Let us now define α_i for $i = 1, \ldots n$, as follows:

$$\alpha_i = -2 \log_e p_i .$$

Clearly the α_i's are independent of each other and each α_i will have a density function g given by:

$$\begin{aligned} g(\alpha_i) = f(p_i)\frac{\mathrm{d}p_i}{\mathrm{d}\alpha_i} &= \frac{1}{2}e^{-\frac{1}{2}di} \text{ for } \alpha \geqslant o, (i = 1, \ldots n) \\ &= o \text{ otherwise.} \end{aligned}$$

for $i = 1, \ldots n$; o otherwise.

Thus α_i has a χ^2 distribution with 2 degrees of freedom.

Let
$$\alpha = \sum_1^n \alpha_i = -2\sum_1^n \log_e p_i(k_i).$$

Since the α_i's are independent and each has a χ^2 distribution with 2 degrees of freedom, α will have a χ^2 distribution with $2n$ degrees of freedom.

What we shall call the α-test simply applies a standard χ^2 test to

$$\alpha = -2 \sum_{1}^{n} \log_e p_i (k_i).$$

In this book the α-test is applied as follows. We take n industry regressions, from which we derive n estimates $\hat{Z}_{\min}$ of $Z_{\min}$. On the basis of these n different values of $\hat{Z}_{\min}$ we wish to test, assuming the errors to be normally distributed, the hypothesis H_0 that all n actual values of $Z_{\min}$ equal zero.

We know that, if H_0 is correct and the errors are normally distributed, $k_i (= \hat{Z}_{\min}/\sigma\, \hat{z}_{\min})_i$ will have a t-distribution with the appropriate degrees of freedom. We can, therefore, calculate $p_i(k_i) = P(t_i \leqslant k_i)$ for each i. Clearly $p_i(k_i)$ is the probability, given H_0 and normality, of observing a t-value not greater than that actually observed.

To apply the test all we do now is calculate

$$\alpha = -2 \sum_{1}^{n} \log_e p_i (k_i)$$

and consult the tabulated significance levels of the χ^2 distribution with $2n$ degrees of freedom.

Let us take, as a concrete example, the regressions based upon the full sample of US firms using unadjusted data. The rounded values of k_i, $p(k_i)$, $-\log_e(p_i)$ obtained are given in Table 30.

Table 30 *The α-test: an example*

Industry	k_i	$p_i(k_i)$	$-\log_e p_i(k_i)$
1	–0.29	0.39	0.95
2	–1.56	0.06	2.73
3	–2.30	0.02	4.09
4	–0.06	0.48	0.74
5	–2.03	0.04	3.31
6	0.28	0.61	0.49
7	–0.78	0.22	1.52
8	–0.43	0.34	1.09
9	–0.19	0.43	0.85

$$\alpha = -2 \sum_{1}^{n} \log_e p_i (k_i) = 31.54.$$

The probability of a χ^2 variable with 18 degrees of freedom having a value less than 31.54 is more than 97.5 per cent. Thus, given the hypothesis H_0, less than one time out of forty would we observe an α as great as that actually observed. Thus we may reject H_0 at the 2.5 per cent level.

The test as it stands is a one-tailed test in the sense that it leads us to reject the null hypothesis only if the observed outcomes k_i are sufficiently negative. Large positive values of k_i never lead to rejection. We can, therefore, test whether a given collection of k's are significantly negative. We cannot test whether they are significantly positive. Fortunately, this omission is easily rectified by replacing the cumulative distribution functions F_i by a new set G_i where

$$G_i(k_i) = 1 - F_i(k_i) = P(t_i > k_i) \quad (i = 1 \ldots n).$$

We then define $p_i(k_i) = G_i(k_i)$ for each i and proceed as before. If the outcomes k_i are sufficiently positive

$$\alpha = -2 \sum_{1}^{n} \log_e p_i(k_i)$$

will be large and the null hypothesis rejected.

To test the hypothesis that the observed values k_i are neither significantly negative nor significantly positive we simply combine these two tests.

It is interesting to note that this test can be used with *any* set of cumulative distributions F_i provided thay are *known* and continuous.

Appendix 3
Size and growth: the functional form

Size and growth: the functional form

In Chapter 3 we saw it was necessary to make some assumption about the form of the relationship between size and growth. The two basic forms used are given by the following equations:

$$g = \text{constant} + \text{dummies} + cS + dS^2 + u \quad (1)$$

$$g = \text{constant} + \text{dummies} + c\log S + d\log^2 S + u \quad (2)$$

For a given constant and set of dummies, each of these results in a U-shaped curve relating g to S. When d is positive U will be upright, when d is negative it will be inverted.

It may happen that, over the observed range of sizes, the curve either rises uniformly or falls uniformly. This will be so if the turning point lies outside the range of observations. Indeed, it may happen that two curves, one U-shaped upwards and one U-shaped downwards, lead to much the same relationship between g and S over the range of sizes covered by the sample. In Fig. 10, for example, a curve which is U-shaped downwards with a very small turning point is, over the middle range, not very different from a curve which is U-shaped upwards with a very large turning point. Thus to compare two curves we need to know whether they are U-shaped upwards or downwards, and where their turning points lie.

With this in mind Table 31 shows the results of fitting each type of curve to the full sample of adjusted data for the years 1962–7. The columns labelled A show the results when the size variables are S and S^2, and those labelled B when they are $\log S$ and $\log^2 S$.

To test which of the functions gives the best fit and, therefore, the most statistically significant relationship between g and S, we used an F-test. In most cases there is not much difference between the two values of F. Where the difference is substantial (chemicals, oil, electrical) the logarithmic form of the equation gives a better fit. Much the same is true for other time-periods and other samples. As a rule, $\log S$ performs slightly better than S.

When the shapes and turning points of the two sets of curves are compared we find a fairly close agreement. In every case but engineering both curves have the same shape – either both are U-shaped upwards, or both are U-shaped downwards – and their turning points are fairly close together. Moreover, in the case of engineering, the U-shaped downwards curve (S) has a turning point at \$2 billion, and the U-shaped upwards curve ($\log S$) has one at \$130 million. There was no firm in engineering with sales in 1962 as low as \$130 million, nor as high as \$2 billion. Thus both turning points lie outside the range covered

Table 31 *The effects of size on growth rates: a comparison*

Industry	R^2		Significance of size		U-Shaped upwards (+) or downwards (–)		Turning point	
	A	*B*	*A*	*B*	*A*	*B*	*A*	*B*
Food	0.161	0.149			–	–	0.46	0.24
Chemicals	0.171	0.208	++	*	+	+	3.14	1.73
Oil	0.167	0.421		*	+	+	5.89	2.12
Iron and steel	0.657	0.669		+	+	+	2.38	1.46
Non-ferrous	0.677	0.655	*	*	+	+	0.72	1.07
Engineering (ex. electrical)	0.339	0.338			+	–	2.00	0.13
Electrical	0.289	0.312	+	++	+	+	3.76	3.20
Autos	0.312	0.312			–	–	–ve	0.00
Miscellaneous	0.067	0.065	+	+	–	–	–ve	0.02
All industries	0.231	0.254	**	**	+	+	7.98	3.17

Notes. A = 1962–7 full sample, adjusted data. (Size variables = S, S^2). B = 1962–7 full sample, adjusted data. (Size variables = $\log S$, $\log^2 S$)

Significance, F-test ** = significant at 1% level; * = significant at 5% level; ++ = significant at 10% level; + = significant at 25% level.

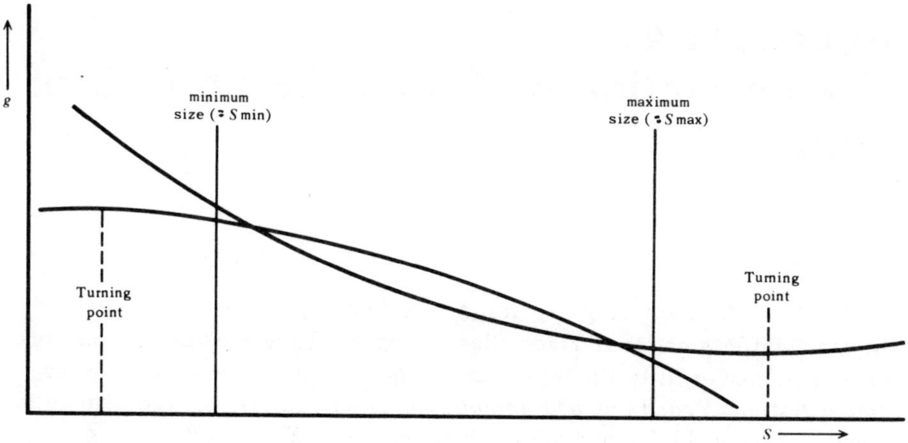

Fig. 10

by the sample, and the curves conform to assumptions underlying Fig. 10. They both slope uniformly downwards over the entire range of observation.

This evidence of similarity is incomplete. Two curves with identical turning points and similar shapes could differ considerably over the sample range. One curve might be much flatter than the other. To see whether this was so, a number of points on each of the curves were computed and compared. There did not seem to be any great differences.

In view of the similarity of the two sets of curves, at least over the range of observation, it is natural to base the analysis on the set which gives the most statistically significant results. Therefore, the logarithmic form, which often provides a better fit than its alternative, and nowhere performs substantially worse, was chosen.

Appendix 4
The derivation of Tables 22 and 23 of Chapter 7

Table 22

Column (1). Manufacturing exports (X) are those goods in categories 5–8 of the Standard International Trade Classification. They are valued f.o.b. and have been converted to US dollars using the exchange rates given by the United Nations *Year Book of International Trade Statistics.* The change in exports between 1957 and 1965 is given by $\Delta X = X^{65} - X^{57}$.

These figures refer not to exports of nationally-owned firms but to those of all firms operating in the country concerned. By including the exports of foreign-owned subsidiaries the importance of foreign markets in expansion is overstated. In most cases, however, the error is unlikely to be large. Exceptions are Canada and Britain. In 1965 nearly half of Canadian exports were produced by US-owned subsidiaries (*Survey of Current Business,* November 1966). For Britain the proportion was 17 per cent.

Column (2). The change in the sales of overseas manufacturing subsidiaries (ΔO) has been estimated from direct investment as follows. Let the sales in any given year t be equal to O^t and let direct investment in manufacturing be I_m^t. Assume that, on average, an investment overseas in manufacturing of one dollar is followed by a permanent increase in the sales in future years of α dollars. If α remains constant the following relationship holds for all values of t,

$$O^{t+1} - O^t = \alpha I_m^t. \tag{1}$$

Assume that I_m^t is a constant fraction β of total direct investment I^t. Then (1) can be written as,

$$O^{t+1} - O^t = \alpha\beta I^t. \tag{2}$$

Or, writing $\gamma = \alpha\beta$,

$$O^{t+1} - O^t = \gamma I^t. \tag{3}$$

Since γ is assumed to be constant, each side of equation (3) can be summed over the years 1957–64 to give,

$$O^{65} - O^{57} = \sum_{t=57}^{64} (O^{t+1} - O^t) = \gamma \sum_{t=57}^{64} I^t. \tag{4}$$

Let us assume that γ is the same for every country, or, to be more specific, is equal to the value of γ for the United States ($= \gamma_{US}$). Then equation (4) become

$$O^{65} - O^{57} = \gamma_{US} \sum_{t=57}^{64} I^t. \tag{5}$$

Thus to estimate $O^{65} - O^{57}$ ($= \Delta O$) we need to know γ_{US} and total direct investment during the years 1957–64.

Estimates of direct investment are given by Marcus Diamond, 'Trends in the Flow of international Private Capital, 1957–65' (*IMF Staff Papers,* March 1967). The value of γ_{US} was estimated by using the US Department of Commerce figure for sales of US manufacturing subsidiaries overseas and Diamond's figure for US direct investment.

Because Diamond's figure for UK investment excludes petroleum it is likely that the estimate of ΔO for the UK is too low.

Column (3). Total overseas sales (P) were assumed to equal exports (X) plus the sales of overseas subsidiaries (O). Imports into the home country from overseas subsidiaries were ignored. The error is not likely to be large as manufacturing, unlike mining and petroleum, subsidiaries do not usually send much of their output back to the home country. American manufacturing subsidiaries, for example, exported roughly 4 per cent of their output back to the US in 1965 (*Survey of Current Business,* November 1966).

Because the figure for the change in exports ΔX of Canadian firms is too high, it is likely that ΔP is also too high. In the case of Britain, on the other hand, errors may have offset each other. As we have already explained, ΔX has been overstated. The change in overseas production ΔO, on the other hand, has probably been understated. If the two errors are equal the result will be a correct estimate of ΔP ($= \Delta X + \Delta O$), but an incorrect breakdown of ΔP into ΔX and ΔO.

Column (4). Total sales S were calculated as follows. Let E be the total sales of manufactured goods produced in the home economy. Part of these goods O^* are produced by foreign-owned subsidiaries. The remainder $E - O^*$ are produced by domestically-owned firms. These firms also sell goods worth O, produced by their overseas subsidiaries. Thus their total sales are equal to those they produce at home $E - O^*$ and those they produce abroad O, i.e.

$$S = (E - O^*) + O = E + (O - O^*). \tag{6}$$

Thus

$$\Delta S = \Delta E + \Delta(O - O^*). \tag{7}$$

Let incoming investment be denoted by I^*, and assume that the same relationship holds between incoming investment and sales, as between outgoing investment and sales. Then, corresponding to equation (3), we have,

$$O^{*t+1} - O^{*t} = \gamma I^{*t}. \tag{8}$$

Thus, summing,

$$O^{*65} - O^{*57} = \gamma \sum_{t=57}^{64} I^{*t}. \tag{9}$$

Taking (9) from (4) we get

$$\Delta(O - O^*) = \Delta O - \Delta O^*$$

$$= \gamma \sum_{t=57}^{64} I^t - \gamma \sum_{t=57}^{64} I^{*t}$$

$$= \gamma \sum_{t=57}^{64} (I^t - I^{*t}). \tag{10}$$

Assuming γ takes the value calculated above, we may use Diamond's figures for net investment $(I^t - I^{*t})$ to estimate $\Delta(O - O^*)$.

All that remains is to estimate ΔE. This was done on the basis of figures for value-added in manufacturing given by *OECD National Accounts.* These were converted to US dollars using official exchange rates. It was then assumed that the ratio of sales E to value-added V was a constant r which varied neither over time, nor from country to country. Given this assumption, the following equations hold,

$$E = rV \tag{11}$$

$$\Delta E = r\Delta V \tag{12}$$

Since V was known, all that remained was to find r. This was estimated by using the 1965 values of E and V for the US, which were both obtainable from US Department of Commerce publications.

Table 23

Column (1). Imports X^* are given c.i.f. by the UN. These were converted to f.o.b. by multiplying by the factor 0.89, which is the ratio of US imports valued f.o.b. to US imports valued c.i.f. in 1969.

Column (4). In deriving E^{65} from value-added, it was necessary to estimate manufacturing value-added for the Netherlands and France. This was done by assuming that the ratio of manufacturing value-added to total GNP was the same in 1967 as it had been in 1965 for the Netherlands and in 1966 for France. For these years the OECD gives figures.

For the meaning of other symbols see Table 22 making the appropriate substitutions of '1967' for '1965' where necessary.

Notes

Chapter 1

1. Petroleum investments in advanced countries consist mainly of refining and distributing facilities.

2. Christopher Layton, *Transatlantic Investment,* The Atlantic Institute, Paris, 1967.

3. J.-J. Servan-Schreiber, *Le défi americain,* Denoel, 1967.

4. Christopher Layton, *European Advanced Technology,* George Allen & Unwin Ltd, 1969.

5. Comprehensive surveys of the literature on size and growth are given by J. Eatwell, 'Growth, Profitability and Size: the Empirical Evidence' in *The Corporate Economy,* ed. R. L. Marris, Macmillan (forthcoming) and Lars Engwall, *Size Distributions of Firms,* Department of Business Administration Stockholm University, 1970.

6. Suppose the size of a firm at time t is S_t, The law of proportionate effect states that,

$$\frac{S_t}{S_{t-1}} = \epsilon_t, \tag{1}$$

where ϵ is a random variable whose distribution is independent S_{t-1}. Taking logs and putting $u_t = \log \epsilon_t$, we obtain,

$$\log S_t = \log S_{t-1} + u_t. \tag{2}$$

Since this equation is valid for all values of t, we get

$$\log S_t = \log S_0 + u_t + u_{t-1} + \dots + u_1. \tag{3}$$

Provided the u's satisfy certain general conditions and are independent of each other, the Central Limit Theorem ensures the sum

$$v_t = u_t + u_{t-1} + \dots + u_1$$

is asymptotically normally distributed. Furthermore, under these general conditions, the variance of v_t increases indefinitely as t increases, so that the initial distribution of S_0 becomes comparatively less important and the distribution of log S_t comes to resemble that of v_t, which itself converges to a normal distribution as t tends to infinity. Moreover, since the variance of v_t tends to infinity, as t tends to infinity, the variance of log S_t also tends to infinity. This implies that the level of concentration increases indefinitely over time.

7. R. Rowthorn and S. Hymer 'The Multinational Corporation: The Non-American Challenge' in *The International Corporation,* ed. by C. P. Kindleberger, Harvard, 1970.

Chapter 2

1. Ranked according to their sales. To qualify as 'industrial' a firm must derive at least 50 per cent of its revenue from manufacturing and/or mining.

2. There were, in fact, 301 US firms as large as the 200th non-US firm but the 301st 'died' during the period. The final sample is, therefore, the same as if 300 rather than 301 firms had been taken.

3. By industry there were 5 food, 3 chemicals, 1 iron and steel, 1 engineering (ex. electrical), and 7 miscellaneous.

4. Unilever was classified as a chemical firm. Tests indicated that transferring it to food would have made no difference to the results.

5. Tests in which iron and steel and non-electrical engineering were regarded as one industry left results unaffected.

6. Unilever and Royal Dutch/Shell are 50 per cent and 40 per cent British respectively. Because of their greater dependence on the UK market than upon the Dutch market, and because of their greater dependence on British political power they are regarded as British. Tests indicated that to have classified them as Dutch would not have made a great difference to the results.

7. It has been found by A. Singh and G. Whittington in *Growth, Profitability and Valuation* (Cambridge University Press. 1968) that amongst UK quoted companies in the period 1954–60 'there was a pronounced tendency for a higher proportion of large firms to revalue' (p. 90). They suggest that this may be one of the reasons why J. M. Samuels (*Review of Economic Studies,* 1965) found that large companies grew faster than small companies. How far such a conclusion would apply in this case is a matter of speculation.

8. Cf. M. A. Adelman, 'The Measurement of industrial concentration', *The Review of Economics and Statistics,* Nov. 1951, pp. 272.

Chapter 3

1. $\log(1+g) = g - \frac{1}{2}g^2 + \frac{1}{3}g^3 \ldots$. When g is small this is approximately equal to g.

2. The term $C \log S$ implies that if one firm is double the size of another then this item will be greater for the bigger firm by an amount $C \log 2$; the term $d \log^2 S$ implies that this item will be greater for the bigger firm by an amount $d \log^2 2 + 2\,d \log 2.\log S$, where S is the size of the smaller firm.

3. The legitimacy of this step can be seen from the fact that each firm comes from exactly one country, and exactly one industry.

Therefore, $\sum_1^m C_i = 1$ and $\sum_1^n I_j = 1$

Thus:

$$(\alpha_1 + \beta_n) + \sum_2^m a_i C_i + \sum_1^{n-1} b_j I_j =$$

$$\alpha_1 \sum_1^m C_i + \beta_n \sum_1^n I_j + \sum_2^m (\alpha_i - \alpha_l) C_i + \sum_1^{n-1} (\beta_j - \beta_n) I_j,$$

the right-hand side of which, after manipulation, reduces to:

$$\sum_1^m \alpha_i C_i + \sum_1^n \beta_j I_j,$$

which are just the terms appearing in equation (3) in the text.

The rewriting of Equation (3) in this way is made necessary by the linear dependence of the set of variables $(C_1 \ldots C_m, I_1 \ldots I_n)$ which are related by the linear equation

$$\sum_1^m C_i - \sum_1^n I_j = 0.$$

To eliminate this dependence it is necessary to reduce the number of explanatory variables by one. This we did by replacing the linearly dependent set $(C_1, \ldots C_m, I_1, \ldots I_n, \log S, \log^2 S)$ by the linearly independent set $(1, C_2, \ldots C_m, I_1, \ldots I_{n-1}, \log S, \log^2 S)$. In other words, we dropped the dummy C_1 of the US and I_n of miscellaneous, and added the constant 1 (unity).

4. The Z corresponding to any other S is given by:

$$Z = c + 2d \log S = tZ_{\text{min}} + (1-t) Z_{\text{max}}$$

where $$t = \frac{\log S_{\text{max}} - \log S}{\log S_{\text{max}} - \log S_{\text{min}}}$$

Clearly, $0 \leqslant t \leqslant 1$ if and only if $S_{min} \leqslant S \leqslant S_{max}$. Thus when S lies between S_{min} and S_{max}, Z lies between Z_{min} and Z_{max}.

5. It is evident that the disturbances are independent of each other and the matrix $E(u\,u')$ is therefore diagonal. If the variances are not identical the ordinary least squares estimators will be unbiassed, but will not be the linear estimators with minimum variance. More to the point, the conventional significance tests may be unreliable.

To see how far variances differed from industry to industry and from country to country, the adjusted growth rates of firms in the full sample were examined. The variance of growth rates was calculated for all the firms of each country and for all the firms of each industry. Bartlett's *M*-test was used to see if variances differed significantly (see *Biometrika Tables for Statisticians*, Vol. 1, E. S. Pearson and H. O. Hartley, Cambridge 1954, p. 57). The values of *M* were statistically significant at the 5 per cent level, but not at the 1 per cent level, for both the industry and country variances. In the country case the lack of uniformity of the variances seemed to be due to the very low variance of Benelux growth rates. If the eight Benelux firms are excluded the variances become remarkably uniform.

These tests are inadequate in one important respect. When the variances were calculated for each industry, for example, it was not possible to take into account the fact that the average size of firm differed from industry to industry, nor that the proportion of firms from each country differed. Part of the difference in calculated variances is due, therefore, to country and size effects. If these were removed it is unlikely that variances would differ significantly from industry to industry. Equally, it is unlikely that variances differ significantly from country to country. In fact, when both industry and country variances are combined and Bartlett's *M*-test is repeated, a procedure which is not strictly legitimate, no trace of any significant differences in variance is found.

There is a substantial body of theoretical and empirical literature which suggests that the variance of growth rates diminishes with the size of firms. To allow for this possibility three different relationships between variance σ^2 and size S were assumed: $\sigma^2 = a$, $\sigma^2 = aS^{-1/2}$, $\sigma^2 = aS^{-1}$. Weighted regressions corresponding to each of these assumptions were then made and the results compared (see A. Goldberger, *Econometric Theory*, Wiley 1964, p.235). There were no substantial differences.

6. These results can be proved using the formulae and proofs given in J. Johnston, *Econometric Methods*, McGraw Hill, 1963, p.p.111–2. Using his notation, let $\boldsymbol{\beta}$ be the least squares estimator of the vector $\boldsymbol{\beta}$ in the equation,

$$\mathbf{Y} = \mathbf{X}\boldsymbol{\beta} + \mathbf{u}.$$

The matrix $\mathbf{X}$ is assumed to consist of fixed elements.

For any vector $\mathbf{C}$, the product $\mathbf{C}'\hat{\boldsymbol{\beta}}$ is an unbiassed estimator $\mathbf{C}'\boldsymbol{\beta}$ provided $E(\mathbf{u}) = 0$. Further, if the disturbances u are independent and have identical variances, i.e. if $E(\mathbf{u}\,\mathbf{u}') = \sigma^2 I$, then $\mathbf{C}'\hat{\boldsymbol{\beta}}$ will have a variance at least as small as that of any other unbiassed linear estimator.

Finally, if the disturbances are normally distributed, the variable

$$t = \frac{\mathbf{C}'\hat{\boldsymbol{\beta}} - \mathbf{C}'\boldsymbol{\beta}}{\hat{s}\sqrt{\mathbf{C}'(\mathbf{X}'\mathbf{X})^{-1}\mathbf{C}}}$$

will have a t-distribution, where $\hat{s}^2$ is the estimated variance of the disturbances, equal to Σ (residuals)^2/degrees of freedom.

The variable t may be re-expressed as follows. Since $\hat{s}^2$ is a scalar,

$$\begin{aligned} \hat{s}^2\,\mathbf{C}'(\mathbf{X}'\mathbf{X})^{-1}\mathbf{C} &= \mathbf{C}'\,(\hat{s}^2\,(\mathbf{X}'\mathbf{X})^{-1})\,\mathbf{C} \\ &= \mathbf{C}'\,\hat{\mathbf{V}}\,(\hat{\boldsymbol{\beta}})\,\mathbf{C}, \end{aligned}$$

where $\hat{\mathbf{V}}(\hat{\boldsymbol{\beta}})$ is the usual least-squares estimate of the variance – covariance matrix of $\hat{\boldsymbol{\beta}}$.

Thus

$$t = \frac{\mathbf{C}'\hat{\boldsymbol{\beta}} - \mathbf{C}'\boldsymbol{\beta}}{\sqrt{[\mathbf{C}'\,\hat{\mathbf{V}}(\hat{\boldsymbol{\beta}})\,\mathbf{C}]}}$$

To apply these results to our own problem we need only notice that:

$$\begin{aligned} Z &= c + 2d\log S = \mathbf{C}'\boldsymbol{\beta}, \\ \hat{Z} &= \hat{c} + 2\hat{d}\log S = \mathbf{C}'\hat{\boldsymbol{\beta}}, \end{aligned}$$

where

$$\begin{aligned} \boldsymbol{\beta}' &= (e,\ a_2,\ \ldots\ a_m,\ b_1\ \ldots\ b_{n-1},\ c,\ d), \\ \hat{\boldsymbol{\beta}}' &= (\hat{e},\ \hat{a}_2,\ \ldots\ \hat{a}_m,\ \hat{b}_1\ \ldots\ \hat{b}_{n-1},\ \hat{c},\ \hat{d}), \\ \mathbf{C}' &= (0,\ \ldots\ 0,\ 1,\ 2\log S). \end{aligned}$$

The expression $\mathbf{C}'\,\hat{\mathbf{V}}\,(\hat{\boldsymbol{\beta}})\,\mathbf{C}$ can be evaluated by expanding,

$$[0,\ \ldots\ 0,\ 1,\ 2\log S]\begin{bmatrix} . & . & . & . \\ . & . & . & . \\ . & . & . & . \\ . & \hat{V}(\hat{c}) & \hat{\mathrm{Cov}}(\hat{c},\hat{d}) \\ . & \hat{\mathrm{Cov}}(\hat{c},\hat{d}) & \hat{V}(\hat{d}) \end{bmatrix}\begin{bmatrix} 0 \\ \vdots \\ 0 \\ 1 \\ 2\log S \end{bmatrix}$$

which is evidently equal to,

$$\hat{V}(\hat{c}) + 4\log S\,\hat{\mathrm{Cov}}(\hat{c},\hat{d}) + 4\log^2 S\,\hat{V}(\hat{d}),$$

which is, of course, equal to the $\hat{V}(\hat{Z})$ given in equation (13) of the text.

Thus

$$t = \frac{\mathbf{C}'\hat{\boldsymbol{\beta}} - \mathbf{C}\boldsymbol{\beta}}{\sqrt{[\mathbf{C}'\,\hat{\mathbf{V}}\,(\hat{\boldsymbol{\beta}})]}} = \frac{\hat{Z} - Z}{\sqrt{[\hat{V}(\hat{Z})]}}$$

has a t-distribution.

Chapter 4

1. Table 12 of the next chapter gives a wider selection.

2. See Table 8.

3. The values of the Spearman rank correlation coefficients r were -0.067 for the Z_{min}'s, 0.167 for the Z_{max}'s, and 0.05 for the F's. None of these is significantly different from zero at the 20 per cent level. Strictly speaking, we should have adjusted the F's to take account of the different degrees of freedom. It is unlikely, however, that such an adjustment would have made any difference.

4. See note 3.

Chapter 6

1. The looseness of this expression springs from the fact that the number of firms may change through time. If this happens the 'average' firm will not grow at the same rate as the total sales or output of all firms combined.

2. See Appendix 4.

3. See Appendix 4.

4. See Appendix 4.

5. Japan, Germany and France were neither substantial importers nor substantial exporters of manufacturing capital before 1957 and for them, therefore, o/S in 1957 was very small. Since $\Delta o/\Delta S$ was also very small, the difference $(\Delta o/\Delta S) - (o/S)$ must have been small. Britain, the Netherlands and the US were substantial net exporters of manufacturing capital before 1957 and for them, therefore, o/S in 1957 was positive and probably not very different from the value of $\Delta o/\Delta S$ during 1957–67. For Italy both inflows and outflows of manufacturing capital before 1957 were small, although on balance the net flow was probably inwards. Thus, o/S was probably negative in 1957, although rather smaller than $\Delta o/\Delta S$ for 1957–67 (-0.07). Thus, $(\Delta o/\Delta S) - (o/S)$ must have been negative, perhaps in the region of -0.04, giving a value of $\Delta S/S$ equal to 0.96 $(\Delta E/E)$

   In assessing the validity of this qualitative argument it is necessary to bear in mind that we need only a very rough idea of the value of o/S. Suppose, for example, that o/S for Italy lies somewhere between -0.02 and -0.12. Then $\Delta S/S$ will lie between 0.95 $(\Delta E/E)$ and 1.05 $(\Delta E/E)$. In other words, for a wide range of values of o/S, $\Delta S/S$ is close to $\Delta E/E$.

6. This value has been estimated in the same way as $\Delta o/\Delta S$, on the basis of figures for direct investment given in the *Statistical Summary Supplement* for 1964 published by the Bank of Canada (Ottawa, 1965).

7. *US Business Investments in Foreign Countries,* US Dept. of Commerce, Washington, 1960.

8. *Effects of UK Direct Investment Overseas.* W.B. Reddaway, Cambridge, 1967.

9. For a discussion of concentration in the United States see Chapter 7.
Evidence for Britain is provided by a report of the Monopolies Commission *General Observations on Mergers* (HMSO, London, 1969). The share of the twenty-eight largest manufacturing firms, ranked according to their net assets, rose from 39 per cent of net assets in manufacturing at the end of 1960 to 50 per cent at the end of 1968. Unfortunately, these statistics do not give a very good picture of what has happened to the share of domestic production accounted for by any constant population of domestically-owned firms. The reasons are:

   (1) The population of twenty-eight firms was not the same at the end of the period as at the beginning.
   (2) Although most of their overseas subsidiaries were excluded, some overseas assets were included.
   (3) Some of the twenty-eight are foreign owned.
   (4) Non-quoted companies were not included. Their share of domestic production may have changed during the period.

   Despite these qualifications, however, it seems likely that the increase in the share of top twenty-eight reflects some genuine increase in the domestic share of the biggest domestically-owned firms.

10. See Chapter 2.

11. Value-added in manufacturing and mining is not a perfect index since it excludes petroleum, Moreover, it is a production rather than sales measure. If goods are unsold the two will diverge, as indeed they will if the degree of vertical integration changes.

Chapter 7

1. *La documentation francaise,* Paris, 1969.

2. These have been calculated on the assumption that inventory changes can be neglected.

3. Least squares regressions of each set of *d*'s on the corresponding set for the preceding time period gave the following results,

$$d_E^{62-65} = 26.7 + 0.74\, d_E^{57-62} \quad R^2 = 0.692$$

$$d_c^{62-65} = 2.4 - 0.01\, d_c^{57-62} \quad R^2 = 0.001$$

$$d_o^{62-65} = 33.4 - 0.15\, d_o^{57-62} \quad R = 0.035$$

4. See note 3.

5. See note 2.

6. These high values of d_O reflect the fact that the seven industries were chosen because they were known to be heavy investors. If all industries had been included some of the values of d_O would have been near zero and the correlation between one-time period and the next would have been positive.

Conclusions

1. The remainder of this chapter merely repeats the Summaries of Chapters 6 and 7.

Department of Applied Economics Occasional Paper Number 12

Effects of U.K. Direct Investment Overseas An Interim Report

W.B. Reddaway
in collaboration with S.J. Potter *and* C.T. Taylor

Cloth 40s. net; Paper covers 25s. net, U.K. prices

and

Department of Applied Economics Occasional Paper Number 15

Effects of U.K. Direct Investment Overseas Final Report

W.B. Reddaway
in collaboration with S.J. Potter *and* C.T. Taylor

Cloth 40s. net; Paper covers 25s. net, U.K. prices

The two Reports make a permanent contribution to the theoretical analysis of the effects of overseas investment, as well as providing guidance of the highest relevance to immediate practical problems. The books are of importance to British companies investing overseas, to students and teachers of economics and to everyone interested in current issues of public policy.

'This is a massive piece of research work whose originality and thoroughness must merit great respect.'

Reginald Maudling in the *Director*

'The Reports are characterised throughout by competence and intellectual sophistication.'

Journal of Economical Literature

Department of Applied Economics Occasional Paper Number 16

Productivity and Capital Expenditure in Retailing

K.D. George
in collaboration with P.V. Hills

A report commissioned by the Economic Development Committee for the Distributive Trades.

The book examines the extent of changes in labour productivity from 1960 to 1966 and assesses the importance of capital in producing these changes. The analysis refers to the operations of firms as a whole and also to case studies relating to different types of projects. These include conversions to self-service, extensions, re-fittings and new shops, and the capital expenditure involved in each case is related to the associated gain in productivity and profits.

Other material includes an examination of the main obstacles to the growth of retail firms, methods of investment appraisal, and the effect of fiscal investment incentives on capital expenditure decisions.

The book is of importance to retailers, to students of economics and to all those interested in issues of policy relating to the service industries.

Paper covers U.K. price 15s. net

Department of Applied Economics Occasional Paper Number 17

Productivity in Transport

A Study of Employment, Capital, Output, Productivity and Technical Change

B.M. Deakin

and

T. Seward

An empirical study of productivity between 1952 and 1965 in six sectors of public transport and communication in the United Kingdom: railways, public road passenger transport, road haulage contracting, sea transport, port and inland water transport, air transport and postal services and telecommunications.
Productivity movements are shown both in terms of output per man and per manhour and also of output per unit of combined labour and capital input. The book tackles such questions as : What has been the productivity performance of these sectors of the public transport industry in the post-war period, taking account of changes in both labour and capital employed? How important are changes in capital per man in explaining changes in output per man? What is the significance of capacity utilization for productivity? When productivity increases relatively fast do prices for the service concerned move down, or move up relatively slowly?
Of interest to all concerned with transport policy as well as to students of economics.

Paper covers 25s.; Cloth 45s. net U.K. prices

Department of Applied Economics Occasional Paper Number 21

The Monopolies Commission in Action

Monopolies and Mergers since 1965

Alister Sutherland

A critical assessment of the major reports made by the Monopolies Commission between 1965 and 1968. The study analyses the criteria used, checks for consistency between inquiries, examines the remedies suggested and summarizes the attitude taken to different aspects of monopoly. The Commission is found to have been inconsistent in finding for the monopolist in Flat Glass (Pilkington), while ruling against in Colour Film (Kodak) and in Cellulosic Fibres (Courtauld); and in not objecting to the B.I.C.C.-Pyrotenax merger. Practical suggestions are made for improving the economic analysis in the inquiries; and for policy changes aimed at improving public control both of existing monopolies and of the biggest mergers.

The book is of importance to businessmen and their advisers, to students and teachers of economics and to everyone interested in current issues of public policy.

Paper covers U.K. price 12s. net